Platform Thinking

Platform Thinking

Read the Past. Write the Future.

Daniel Trabucchi and Tommaso Buganza

Leader in applied, concise business books

Platform Thinking: Read the Past. Write the Future.

Copyright © Business Expert Press, LLC, 2023.

Cover design by Daniel Trabucchi and Tommaso Buganza

Interior design by Exeter Premedia Services Private Ltd., Chennai, India

First published in 2023 by
Business Expert Press, LLC
222 East 46th Street, New York, NY 10017
www.businessexpertpress.com

ISBN-13: 978-1-63742-446-9 (paperback)
ISBN-13: 978-1-63742-447-6 (e-book)

Business Expert Press Service Systems and Innovations in Business and Society Collection

First edition: 2023

10 9 8 7 6 5 4 3 2 1

Description

*What does **platform thinking** mean? It is the ability to put platform-based mechanisms at the core of digital business transformations in business.*

Digital platforms like Uber, Spotify, Airbnb, and Booking.com completely reshaped the daily life of millions of users. However, many innovation leaders struggle to conceive the significance of their impact. Platform-based business models are not just the real geeks of startups, digital services, and unicorns.

This book shows that their potential in creating value is higher than suspected.

Even though platform ecosystems are complex, readers will take on a journey to become platform thinkers. Their eyes will be trained to look beyond what's visible and start *reading the platform world* around them. Then, they will be guided into a step-by-step process and learn how to *write* a new platform model from scratch.

This book is the result of a decade of research. It offers both a framework and practical instruments to champion digital transformation in any organization. It is specially intended for those who are interested in the glittering platform world and are still trying to figure it out.

Keywords

platform thinking; innovation; platforms; digital business; data; business transformation; business model; idle asset

Contents

Testimonials

"This book has a clear purpose. It challenges business leaders to think differently and recognize the innovative potential of platform business models and 'platform thinking' more generally. This is particularly prescient message as European platforms have largely lagged the rest of the world. With a deft combination of essential frameworks and highly informative cases, Trabucchi and Buganza will surely inspire a wave of platform formation and innovation."
—**Peter C. Evans, PhD, Chief Strategy Officer, McFadyen Digital, and Co-Chair of the MIT Platform Strategy Summit**

"In a challenging and fast-changing business environment, this book is a must to read for all the executives called to reframe their Company's business model or in search for the innovation Gral. The authors guide the reader through the complex world of the platforms, providing 'new glasses' to see current business under a novel perspective and, if the case, rethink it. Always with the clear goal to stay competitive in the long run."—**Augusto Mitidieri, Executive Director, Switzerland Innovation Park Ticino, multiawarded CEO**

"This book shows entrepreneurs and veteran managers alike how to consider the creation or growth of a multi-sided platform. Those who ignore it will be doubly surprised when a platform recruits their customers and suppliers with a better offer. With hundreds of examples and templates, Trabucchi and Buganza also demonstrate that anyone can—and probably must—build a platform business."—**Ted Ladd, Professor at Hult, Instructor at Harvard and Stanford, author of *Innovating with Impact* from the Economist**

"Daniel Trabucchi and Tommaso Buganza take studies on platforms to a new level: as a way of thinking that may spur innovation whichever business you are in. Read this, and you can turn your own company into a platform, and benefit at most from the power of digitalization."—**Roberto Verganti, Stockholm School of Economics and Harvard Business School, Author of *Design Driven Innovation*, HBS Press**

"All of us, that are working on Digital Business Models, know the difficulties to explain what is a platform, what is the difference between digitalization and being digital, so every time that somebody is making an effort to explain and spread the word about the main characteristics of this kind of business models is a step towards the adoption because if we don't know, we don't choose. On this occasion, I am so glad to see the two authors Tommaso and especially Daniel that I personally know and admire have done this effort, I like how they merge the academic side with the practical side, and in the end, their main expertise as an Academics and Researchers!

A book to discover and understand what we mean when we are talking about the value exchange in a platform, practical use cases Uber, Booking.com, Whatsapp, and most important reinforce the idea of 'Platform Thinking as a mindset"—**Marina Planas, CEO and Founder of TheNTWK**

"Platform Thinking offers a new, original perspective on platforms for established firms that wish to embrace a digital business transformation. We are used to consider platforms either the tech giants, often US based, or creative start ups in the digital space. Trabucchi and Buganza show how platforms can be thought of as paradigm for a much wider range of businesses and help them imagine and build a new bright, and sustainable, future!"—**Francesco Caio, Chairman and CEO**

"Trabucchi and Buganza introduce a new perspective on platform businesses and provide straightforward explanations replete with real world examples. They offer valuable and practical tools for managers creating and interacting with platform businesses. Platform Thinking *is for anyone interested in better understanding the challenges and opportunities of platform businesses."*
—**Elizabeth J. Altman, University of Massachusetts Lowell, Author of** ***Workforce Ecosystems: Reaching Strategic Goals with People, Partners, and Technologies*** **(MIT Press).**

Acknowledgments

Platform Thinking, to us, is not just a book, but is the cornerstone of a long, innovative, and meaningful project—a project made of 30+ scientific papers, the birth of a brand new conference called Symplatform, three Coursera massive online open courses (MOOCs), a Miro toolkit, hundreds of slides, courses, speeches, videos….travels, writing weeks, and coffees.

We didn't start together, but this project got us together.

Tommaso first had an epiphany about platforms in 2012 while running in Central Park during his visiting period at Parson's School for Design. Daniel began this journey listening to Tommaso's class in 2014 and then asking him to collaborate for his master thesis (by the way, now Daniel is a runner too).

Platform Thinking is to us the research project that best fits our way of living the research activity: putting passion in action, studying what gets our attention, positioning the joy of discovering and understanding before any other objective, and, finally, having a real impact on people and organizations around us.

In our journey, we met many people that had a significant and special role.

First of all, we acknowledge the work of all those people that shared with us a piece of this research journey: Elena Pellizzoni, Claudio Dell'Era, and Roberto Verganti who published with us the very first "platform-related" study on Waze back in 2015 and many others that came after. We also thank a lot all the researchers that came later for other studies and published works: Stefano Magistretti, Andrea Patrucco, Silvia Sanasi, Antonio Ghezzi, Antonella Moretto, Alan MacCormack, Federico Frattini, Philip Meier, Matthias Trischler, Luca Gastaldi, Deepak Saxena, Diletta Di Marco, Filomena Canterino, Emilio Bellini, Paola Bellis, Silvia Magnanini, and Federico Zasa.

A special mention here is for Laurent Muzellec and Sebastien Ronteau. They are not just coauthors; they are two friends that first believed in our perspective on platforms and cofounded Symplatform with us.

A huge thanks to our home, LEADIN'Lab: the lab of Leadership, Innovation and Design at the School of Management of Politecnico di Milano. We call it a home because we are like a family sharing not just projects, but also the everyday life, sparkling suggestions, harsh feedbacks, insights, and ideas.

Thanks to the IPDM community, which first welcomed in 2015 the very first paper about data and two-sided platforms; thanks to all the people that nurtured our ideas and let them grow in a safe space. Thanks to Jennie Bjork and Katharina Holtze for believing in our research on the innovation strategies for platforms and our first special issue, Gloria Barczak for supporting our blockchain research, and Paul Caughlan and Abbie Griffin, representing the whole IPDM community, for their nurturing spirit and kindness.

Nothing we wrote in the book would be there without all the platform professionals we met and interviewed over the years. A special thanks must go to Alessandro Cadoni and Matteo Sarzana, who, when all of this was just a fuzzy idea, accepted our interview request: your support throughout the journey has been incredible. Thanks to Francesca Vidali who often joined us to share her (evolving) experience in our classes. Thanks to Alessandro Tommasi and the Will Team for inspiring us with their everyday work and having shared with us their view on the platform world.

Thanks to Augusto Mitidieri for the support on the project and the feedback on the early version of the book.

Thanks to Alessandro Perego who believed in "platform thinking" for the creation of Platform Thinking HUB and was among the early readers of this book.

Thanks to our international platform friends; to Marina Planas and Sabrina Guzman for welcoming us in TheNTWK; and to the networkers who sustain our work: Nicolas Duerr, Maximilian Gutsche, and Alex Pesjak. Thanks to Ted Ladd and Peter Evans who sustained us in the last stages of the development of the book.

A special thanks goes to Francesco Caio who validated much of our work during the hours of "Managing Technology Disruption" course at Politecnico di Milano.

A warm thanks goes to Susana Sancassani who believed in "platform thinking" from the educational point of view and invested in it. Also, a huge thanks goes to the "platform thinking" MOOCs team: Bianca Santolini, Daniela Casiraghi, Federica Brambilla, Francesca Bruschi, Marco Frascarelli, Amedeo Longeri, and Francesco Meroni. Your patience and abnegation was way beyond your duties.

Thanks to the researchers who inspired us the most with their works. Thanks to Rochet and Tirole for giving us the seminal reference and letting us understand the world of two-sided markets. Thanks to Parker and Valstyne, Amit and Zott, Evans, and Hagiu and Wright: your works represented fundamental steps in our understanding of the world of platforms. Thanks to Gawer and Cusumano for showing us the path to link platforms and innovation with their seminal piece on JPIM and thanks to Annabelle for opening the door for conversations and collaborations with us!

Thanks to Business Expert Press and to Scott Isenberg who believed in this project and literally made us walking on air for days. This is just the beginning.

Not only this book but everything we do would just not exist without the support of our families. Supporting two researchers that embrace this kind of project means at least two annoying things. First is giving up a lot of time that could have been spent together. Second is having someone nearby that repeats "platform" a dozen times a day. Thanks to Aline and Clara. Thanks to Ludovica. And also thanks to our whole families: no words are needed; gratitude is the best feeling to express everything.

And finally, the two of us, for overcoming many differences and building something meaningful together—something that goes beyond the book and the research, something that changed us as human beings first. That's what matters the most.

CHAPTER 1

A World That Changed…and the Need for New Glasses

Going Beyond the Obvious: Platforms' Perception

When you land in Rome, it takes a 50-minute taxi ride to go from the airport to the city center. We were heading to the city center for a meeting with a client, and as we always do, we took a cab.

We were in the backseat preparing for our meeting when the driver decided it was time for a small talk. He had spent the previous weekend on the Amalfi coast with his family. Listening to his words, we could clearly visualize the fantastic view of the Mediterranean Sea he had from a cozy, tiny apartment in the middle of Positano. He had spent three days with his wife and two kids there, living at a local's place in Positano exactly as people living there do. Obviously, he was not talking about a hotel, but of an Airbnb. After his experience, he tried to convince us that hotels were the past and we had to use Airbnb instead. It is cozier, more welcoming, and above all cheaper than a hotel room. He even had some friends renting their apartments, just in case we were interested.

When we told him that we studied these companies, he was thrilled and asked for other similar services to use personally and share with friends. But when we mentioned Uber, the atmosphere in the cab changed abruptly.

To be an Airbnb user was terrific for him. Still, as a potential competitor, Uber was a lot less cool. He had several good reasons to consider it unfair, from the type of driving license needed to ride a taxi in Italy to the cost of the compulsory cab license. "Airbnb is right because hotel owners take advantage of the customers offering overpriced services; we [taxi drivers] barely can survive with what we gain," he said.

It was spring 2015; in those days, Uber was rapidly growing in Italy, but several strikes were taking place, even attacking the Italian country manager.

In the beginning, we just considered this double judgment as a textbook case of fundamental attribution error: when we incorrectly attribute a person's actions. For example, when someone cuts us off on the road, we may think it is because of their personality. They are simply no nice people. However, if we cut off somebody else, it is attributed to the situation (something like "I'm a nice person, I never do it…but I was really late and risking losing my flight").

Since then, though, we have slightly but constantly changed our minds.…

Digital platforms are changing our lives in many ways. Take a couple of seconds and picture yourself in the following situations:

1. Calling a cab
2. Ordering a pizza
3. Watching a movie
4. Listening to a song
5. Booking a room in a city you want to visit
6. Running
7. Driving somewhere

We are sure that almost all of them happen through a platform. Calling a cab may be by dialing a number on the phone or more probably through mytaxi, Taxiapp, or any local version of these apps, or through a different kind of cab like Uber or Lyft. Ordering a pizza may be done through JustEat, Uber Eats, Deliveroo, or any other food delivery services. Watching a movie is more and more done through Netflix, Disney+, Prime Video, or similar services. Songs are listened through Spotify, Apple Music, or Tidal. Booking a room is mostly done through Booking.com or Airbnb. Running happens very frequently with the support of services like Runtastic, Nike+ Running, and Runkeeper, while apps like Google Maps or Waze usually support us when driving.

The earlier list is short. They are just seven daily activities. We may go on much more than that. Still, this is not the goal. Let's stop here and think about the previous lines. All those companies are platforms. In different ways and for different reasons, we will have time and space, later, to see why they are platforms and how they work. But there are at least three other points that we need to highlight clearly.

1. If we look back to 2010, not ages ago, we will quickly note that most of the activities taking place on earth would *not* require the support of a platform.
2. We are talking about very general, daily, and worldwide activities.
3. There is a common denominator, the smartphone, the enabling technology for all of this.

This short reflection leads to a straightforward observation: we live in the platform economy that emerged quickly, spread in so many aspects of our daily routine, and is powered by an "ordinary" but powerful object that is often in our hands: the smartphone.

Smartphones represent our gate between a real world and a virtual one, and we cross this border hundreds of times every day.

Besides the specific products or services, platforms like Uber, Spotify, and Amazon changed our whole customer experience. We are accustomed to having personalized and real-time services. Netflix suggests to us what to see, Deliveroo what to eat, and Amazon what to read. The ease of use, convenience, and personalization that characterize these services make them a must-have for many of our daily activities. Platforms providers have been able to challenge some of the most accepted theories of innovation. Rogers, in the 1960s, showed how innovations need time to spread over a broad population, convincing anyone to use a new product (Rogers 2003). These services, in just a few years, convinced everyone literally. Think about how many people now in their 60s, 70s, or 80s use Facebook or WhatsApp, while only a few years ago they used to fight with the "damn mobile phone."

We, as a society, fell in love with these services. As users, we deeply love them. Nevertheless, are we sure that we fully understand them? Or do we only look at them on the surface?

Let's go back to our taxi driver. In his case, probably, he was staying on the surface: appreciating something (Airbnb) as a user and not reasoning anyhow on something remarkably similar (Uber) in his business domain. This is just a first misconception on platforms: everyone likes them as users, but very few like them when they challenge their professional status quo. Even more, many think that platforms can be created only in Silicon Valley or that platforms cannot exist if you are not working in a native digital field.

Our experience is that not only taxi drivers but also managers often do not go beyond the surface. They look at what these platforms do with a naïve customer point-of-view. How often have we heard somebody saying that they wanted to be the Amazon, Uber, or Airbnb of their industry? Uberizing even became a verb! But we are here to discuss a relatively small number of successful platforms right now, which means that a naïve attempt to mimic them can be a bad mistake.

The problem with our taxi driver was not only a fundamental attribution error; he was genuinely unable to recognize the similarities between Airbnb and Uber and grasp their functioning system. Unfortunately, many innovation managers are proving to be equally blind. The digital platform world is not simple at all, and a sign of the greatness of platform leaders is their ability to make it simple for the customer what is complex for them.

The word platform is incredibly abused, and if you ask managers what a platform is (we did it, you'll find the results later), you can get very diversified answers ranging from automotive platforms to operating systems to the App store. The intriguing thing is that all these definitions are correct, which generates even more confusion among the practitioners and academics communities.

The study of platforms challenges us and our innate need to simplify reality to make sense of it. Once we find a good definition fitting the reality, we hardly challenge it. Unfortunately, the concept of platform is far from being simple, univocal, and clear. It is frightening, complicated, and multifaced. We can have product platforms, innovation platforms, transactional platforms, orthogonal platforms, and even others. All these are platforms, and they are not even as new as we could imagine in many cases. Instagram and the *New York Times* are much more similar than most of us can imagine—but we fail to see it if we do not go beyond the service surface and understand their functioning mechanism.

Why Another Book on Platforms? Because It Is a Matter of Absorptive Capacity

This is not the first book about platforms. There are plenty of them. We read most of them, we fell in love with many of them, and we have been inspired by the ones that took on the challenge of talking about platforms before. Annabelle Gawer and Michael Cusumano showed us what platforms are with their fundamentals articles and gave us newer insights with their latest book *The Business of Platforms*. With their *Platform Revolution*, Geoffrey Parker, Marshal Van Alstyne, and Sangeet Paul Choudary inspired us with amazing cases and their wider view on platforms. David Evans and Richard Schmalensee proved to us that focusing on two-sided platforms was a great bet with their *Matchmakers*.

Nevertheless, all these and other books and the articles that we read and do not mention explicitly have a different angle. Many focus on the economic approach to platforms (or "two-sided markets") and are mainly oriented toward the definition and the balancing of the value captured by both sides. The central concept is the network externalities, and their reasonings are about the sensitivity to price and the relative price policies, for example, the decision to subsidize one side delivering a free service for credit card holders and a payment service for merchants.

Another relevant approach to studying platforms is more managerial and based on the business models for creating and capturing value. This approach highlights relevant issues like the chicken-and-egg paradox or the difference between product and innovation platforms. Other studies focus more on the technological dimensions of platforms, and the list may go on. All these contributions are leveraged in this book; we will even summarize some of them, but we promise to focus on something different. We want to focus on people—on those people that can leverage platforms to foster innovation, those managers that can exploit a new way of thinking, or, as we say, "platform thinking."

Platforms are not just a different business model. We claim they are a true enabler for innovation. Platforms are not just a possible way to capture value when you create an innovative product or service, but can, and we claim they should, be leveraged by both startups and established companies to foster future innovations.

In other words, a digital platform-based approach can be a way to capture value once you have a significant innovation, for example, in the Facebook case, when they had excellent service and a huge community but no ways to monetize it. But we argue that a digital platform-based approach can also be an antecedent to innovations, an enabler (as you have an existing platform, you can now create new products and services on top of it).

To take advantage of this enabler, though, we must change our way of seeing the world and understanding the platforms we use every day. We need to develop a clear competence to read and understand the dozens of differences and implications between similar platforms and to be able to see where they are equal instead. To write the future, we need to be able to read the present.

As learners, we need to fill our brains with words and concepts to express new complex messages. We cannot truly aspire to express complex thoughts if we have few categories in mind and an oversimplified understanding of reality. To leverage platforms to foster innovation, we need to learn and understand the language of platforms.

This is what this book is about: we aim to provide the absorptive capacity needed to understand current platforms and their trajectories fully. Then, we propose a concrete process and tools to put your existing business—but also your ideas for new businesses—at the beginning of these trajectories and imagine a roadmap to transform it into a platform-based business.

Absorptive capacity is a keystone in the management and business world. Cohen and Levinthal defined it in 1990 as the "ability to recognize the value of new information, assimilate it, and apply it to commercial ends." Originally it referred to a firm ability, but it is often studied as an individual characteristic. This is what we will do in this journey together: help you to recognize the value of platforms, assimilate it—going beyond the surface—and apply it in your world for innovation purposes.

To Make Something New, We Must Be New

Platforms innovation is not (only) technological innovation; it is a different way of understanding the world. Let's go deeper in this observation through the case of a great innovator: TomTom.

TomTom is a Dutch multinational company founded in 1991. Tom-Tom revolutionized an everyday activity: to drive to an unknown place. If you are old enough, you can probably remember the old maps of roads—the ones that sat unused in the backseat of cars for months, till the moment of the holidays. Some may remember the one big certainty: the extreme difficulty of neatly folding the map back up after using them.

Well, TomTom and other companies like Garmin, which was its main competitor and got prominence in the same years, changed it forever. Their GPS turn-by-turn navigators revolutionized our way of driving: finally, a digital device could tell us where to turn to reach an unknown place. People used to buy the navigator, the maps, and their updates, as they used to buy a video recorder and VHS cassettes. TomTom and its competitors changed the world and achieved massive success with it. Then the world changed again. On July 10, 2008, Steve Jobs announced the App Store, the hub where anyone could provide an app for Apple's latest success: the iPhone.

In 2009, the company promptly identified the possibility of moving toward the emerging app industry enabled by smartphones and App stores. They understood that the smartphone had all the previously embedded hardware into their products (a screen, a GPS antenna, a speaker, and a memory to upload the maps). Hardware technology was becoming a commodity; everyone with a smartphone would have it, but the actual value of their offering was in the software application (including the main asset: the maps).

So, they developed a smartphone app to use the device as a turn-by-turn navigation system. Other similar companies like Garmin did a very similar thing. It was rational, timely, and well done. Unfortunately, they missed two points. The first one is that (especially at those times) the apps were free or they cost few dollars. TomTom was accustomed to asking a significant price for the application and the maps. In 2009, they just replicated the same request on the app stores, leaving the customers confused and puzzled—$99.99 was an incredibly high price on the market.

Moreover, they did not see that the smartphone brought along many more things than just the hardware. Even at those times, the most popular apps were social networks like Facebook. Customers were ready to have networks of users efficiently collaborating, and this allowed the offer of outstanding new services. We used the classic turn-by-turn navigation system provided by TomTom and Garmin to solve a specific problem: to help us reach a place we did not know. New competitors like Waze were free from the legacy of old business models and quickly saw the new potentiality of the smartphone as a platform to connect users. The service could be more pervasive than just supporting you when driving toward unknown places. It could become a companion to solve the most critical driving problem, especially in cities: traffic. The same person could be a user of the system and a contributor also. Even more, she could do it actively (by signaling blocks or traffic of the way) or passively (by letting the system track her speed and relative slowdowns probably due to traffic).

This is called a technology epiphany in contrast to a technology substitution (Verganti 2009). Waze was able to unveil a quiescent service into the smartphone, while TomTom and Garmin were just porting the old business model on a new technology without appreciating the potentialities offered by this new technology (Buganza et al. 2015).

This is not uncommon; it is also called mediamorphosis (Fidler 1997). When dealing with a new medium, we as human beings always start by replicating what we did with the previous one. The first content to be played in movie theaters were theaters plays, and the first contents to be broadcasted on tv were cinema movies. It took time to understand the potentiality of cinemas and, therefore, the possibility of frequently alternating indoor and outdoor scenes to break the temporal line or the incredible power of special effects. Also, it took time for alternative content formats to find their way into the tv sets, such as quiz shows, tv-series, and reality shows.

So, what happened to TomTom and Garmin was nothing new. We already know that a technology substitution in many cases can result in a failure.

But even if this is clear, how to do it is much more complicated. It is a mindset issue. Instead of imprisoning the new world into old frameworks, we should evolve the old business into the new world.

Let us be very clear here. This reasoning started with TomTom, one of the most outstanding examples of an "innovative company" worldwide. They changed people's lives with their GPS turn-by-turn navigators. They also saw the most incredible opportunity of the last decades—smartphones—when it appeared, and leveraged it by launching an app in one year since the announcement of the App Store when very few large companies had done it. Today, TomTom is a leading company in the business-to-business (B2B) mapping services, being, for example, the primary supplier of data for Apple's map app since 2018. They lost a battle but still ruled the innovation war, even though something did not work.

They saw it coming (the app revolution). Now, when it arrived, they leveraged it. They did it greatly (their app was functional, meaningful, and working—when people did not know how to write apps for iPhone). But it was not enough, and someone took their place in that world.

In our opinion, the reason why—ex post—is clear. They took their perfect model and brought it to a new world. The model (the GPS navigator with add-on maps) was great. Still, the world changed abruptly, and it suddenly turned to be old in the world of personalized services and continuous and immediate improvement. They kept their linear value chain in a networked world. They indulged a bit too long in looking at a new world with old eyes.

This is what this book is about: providing you the glasses to see the new world clearly; to see platforms, with all their nuances, as models, to understand them; to develop a new mindset that lets you see the new world, that lets you think in a new way…in two words: platform thinking.

Platforms Are Not Just for Tech and Young Companies

Another misconception that we found many times interacting with managers is the belief that platform equals startup. It is not difficult to understand from where this misconception comes. Many of the so-called Unicorns (startups capitalizing over a billion without being listed) are platforms indeed (Trabucchi et al. 2019). The platform approach, especially in the case of matchmaking platforms like Uber or Airbnb, which allow providers and users to meet and reduce possible frictions between them (first due to the payment systems), is easily scalable. Many of us could see the shocked surprise on the face of people when they were told the value of these companies, and the most common comment was, "That's cool, but they basically do nothing!"

This is not true; they do a lot to create value, and we will talk about it. Still, Uber revolutionized the cab industry without investing a cent in vehicles, and Airbnb heavily shook the world of hotels and accommodation without owning a single bedroom. For these companies which offer match-making and payment services, the platform model proved to be effective to capture the value and almost infinitely scalable. Many startups saw in these models the opportunity to create something new, searching for assets (like drivers' idle time or unused rooms in a house) that had a potential but untapped value on the market. And it worked incredibly well. For many of them, born in the new millennium, these opportunities were crystal clear.

Nevertheless, not everything can be managed by a startup.

The world we are living in often calls for considerable and long-ranged solutions to complex problems. Energy production, mobility, health care systems, and education are only some examples of industries that need a profound redefinition in the upcoming years.

Are these changes coming from startups? It might be, but our belief in this is wavering. Consider, for example, the higher education system and the universities. The "Uber" of high education is yet to come. Remarkable services like Coursera or Lynda impacted the industry, but old-fashioned universities are still up and running. Even the pandemic and all the digital advancements connected to it could not cancel them. Many other sectors are in similar positions.

Startups live under constant pressure of shorter-ism due to their natural need for survival and saw in the platform world a flexible, fast, and scalable way to test business models and increase their chance to survive. So why are established and mature companies still so anchored in a traditionally linear value chain model? Why not leverage the same opportunity? They have the solidity of established firms; they have assets built over the years and less pressure on the short-term goals. They often have innovation in their DNA because they reached their position thanks to their ability to offer something new when they entered the market. Still, they often remain stuck in their old success path, failing to foster the Darwinian evolutionary laws, and remain in an inertia that let other companies to jump in and fly higher (Moore 2008).

Among many variables, what they are certainly missing is the correct mindset. Shifting their mindset toward the world of platforms could open them to innovation avenues that startups cannot pursue and to have a major impact on the world we live in.

In other words, platform thinking is an incredible opportunity. Still, we must stop looking at platforms as a quick, easy-to-scale business model for digital startups. Established firms can leverage platforms as well. Many of them are starting their venture into this world, abandoning the linear business model to embrace a two- or multisided one. Apple can be considered a precursor: a traditional computer manufacturer perfectly described by Porter's value chain (design the products, buy the components, assemble, manage the logistics, and sell the final output), which leverages the platform thinking approach and launches an app store connecting developers in search for clients and users in search for solutions.

To find the future in your existing business, you must shift your mind and reframe the way you look at the world. Innovation opportunities enabled by platforms are all around us. We are just not trained to see them. The Netflix of corporate training or the Uber of gardening are expressions that only mimic something we do not fully grasp and understand. Trying to copy existing models and moving them in a different field is not enough and can be detrimental. Platforms are not only a technological change. Platforms are a new way of conceiving the business ecosystem.

Platform thinking is a new mindset.

Alessandro Baricco, an Italian writer and director, said it ideally in his latest essay, "The game." If we look back in history, all the greatest technical revolutions directly link with a revolution in the mindset and in how people think. He makes a great example of parallelism in the 18th century among the First Industrial Revolution and the Age of Enlightenment.

We live in the era of a substantial technical revolution. The digital revolution changed the world. It changed what we can do, how we can move globally, how we can communicate with others. It changed everything. Still, there has not been a mindset shift of similar magnitude.

This is what we are claiming in the more miniature world of platforms. The technical shift, the model revolution, happened. It is clear, and it is here. Notwithstanding, a comparable shift has not followed it in the mindset of businesspeople. We often see the model, understand it, but still think about linear value chains with suppliers, internal operations, and final customers. This will not be enough to exploit the value of platforms fully. Businesspeople and innovation managers need to start thinking in a new way; they need to develop a "platform [way of] thinking."

This book will teach you how to shift your mindset in the platform world to write the future, but to do it, it will start by training how to read the past, unveiling the peculiarities, and going beyond the surface of the world of platforms.

The Structure of the Book

The book is built around the large metaphor of using platform thinking to read the reality around us and to write the future while fostering innovation now. Therefore, the book is built conceptually around two main parts. The first one aims to show you how to use platforms to read the reality around us, to go beyond the fancy cover of the "platforms" we use every day and to truly understand their peculiarities in terms of value creation and value capturing. Chapters 2 to 4 are in this first part of the book.

Chapter 2—"The history and types of platforms"—offers a comprehensive story of how the concept of platforms entered in the innovation landscape. Going through various cases, it introduces the concepts of product platforms and innovation platforms, as the roots of the field we consider. Then, it builds on the concept of multisided platforms introducing transactional platforms and orthogonal platforms, to conclude with the notion of hybrid platforms.

Chapter 3—"How to design a platform"—looks mainly at transactional platforms aiming to explore the peculiarities that they have in the early days of the platform life: the design. In particular, the chapter explores the value drivers that make relevant the work of the platform providers, to then explore the early challenges (chicken-and-egg paradox, pricing dynamics, launching phase, etc.) that need to be overcome to let the platform live. In the last part of the chapter, the main strategies to let the platform grow and prosper are introduced.

Chapter 4—"The role of data in platform thinking"—brings back orthogonal platforms at the center of the discussion. In particular, the chapter explores the role that data play in the generation of orthogonal platforms through client-as-a-source strategies. The chapter goes through many cases that highlight different strategies to exploit the value embedded in data generated during a digital service. In the last part, the implications of these strategies in terms of privacy concerns and business model transparency are discussed.

The second part of the book, dealing with the ability to write the future of platforms, is made of Chapters 5 to 7. The goal here is to develop platform thinking as the ability to see platforms as a tool for innovation that can be applied to established—linear value chain—organization, transactional platforms, orthogonal platforms, networks, or any kind of existing organization.

Chapter 5—"Platform thinking mindset"—introduces the idea of idle asset hunting as the main capability of the platform thinker, the innovator, that uses the powers of platforms. The chapter is built around four different cases: Booking.com, Chiara Ferragni, WhatsApp, and Amazon, which are analyzed through the lenses of platform thinking, to show how they evolved—from a platform perspective—over the years.

Chapter 6—"The platform thinking process"—puts platform thinking in action by introducing a process that aims to support innovators, by fostering innovation through the lenses of platforms. The process is based on four steps (step back and read, where you are; dive in and read, what you have; dive in and write, where you may go; step back and write, the roadmap to get there) and the relative tools (from existing tools like the Business Model Canvas and the value map, to ad hoc created tools like the Idle Asset Canvas and the Platform Thinking Canvas) that support the generation of ideas and their structuring process to foster platform thinking.

Chapter 7—"What's next, with your new glasses?"—closes the book with a clear and important message: technologies change and evolve so fast that many of these examples will be old soon, but by embracing the platform thinking mindset, we'll be able to find and exploit opportunities in them.

This book is the keystone of a living project made of courses, toolkits, podcasts, videos, Symplatform (our conference), and much more things to come that are partially presented throughout the book (e.g., Chapters 2 to 4 are directly linked to three free courses and Coursera, while the platform thinking process has its own free Toolkit available on Miro). Still, the project is not over. Visit platformthinking.eu (Figure 1.1) to remain updated on the platform thinking world.

Figure 1.1 QR code for PlatformThinking.eu

Source: https://platformthinking.eu/.

CHAPTER 2

The History and Types of Platforms

What Is a Platform? Going Beyond the Buzzword

Platforms are everywhere; "platform" is one of the most used words of the last years, probably of the decade. There are thousands of companies pretending to be a platform. Every day, thousands of journalists call services "platforms" correctly—but also, not so accurately sometimes.

Is there a way to prove this overuse of the word platform?

We can find the answer to this question in the most obvious place where we look for answers: Google.

By writing a single word, "platform," we got 5.87 billion results (in 0.36 seconds, and it could be interesting to repeat this experiment while you are reading it[1]).

Is it a huge number? Is it impressive? Is it lower than our expectations? Well, we have no clue, not until we compare it to a reference point. Let's try to search for other "buzzwords" that we hear in our lectures, that we read in newspapers, and that we hear in the news.

Here are some of them:

- Innovation has 2.18 billion results
- Design thinking 1.36 billion results
- Disruption 0.606 billion results
- Agile 0.433 billion results

Yes, the use of platform as a term is huge!

---

[1] Data were retrieved on February 19th, 2023.

Probably more massive than our expectations. Even though we, as researchers of the topic, spend a significant part of our lives talking about platforms. It's bigger than "innovation," the must-have word of any service launch. It is more than doubling "design thinking," the must-know methodology in the business world. It is far more extensive than "disruption" or "agile," two of the worst used words in the management world.

This is impressive.

But what do people say about platforms? We took two international outlets, *The New York Times* and *Business Insider* and searched for "platform" in their internal search engines.

In *The New York Times*, we found six results over the last day, five and six in the two previous days. Not a bad result for such a generalist outlet. But what are they talking about? Well, the topics are heterogeneous. They move from recent news on Twitter and Facebook and their daily life roles to an in-depth analysis of the 6+ hours "blackout" that Instagram, WhatsApp, and Facebook had just a couple of days before. Another article talks about sexual assault as one of the latest discussion trend that took place on TikTok. The last two news of the day tackle different topics. One is about "Squid Game," the latest smash hit by Netflix, and its impact on Lyst, the shopping platform to find clothes and shoes used in the series. The last one talks about the latest investment by Harry and Meghan and presents "Sustainability for Everyone," a new fintech asset manager platform that scores a person's portfolio along different ethic dimensions.

The discussion seems broad, but it is not as wide as it is. A couple of days back, it was easy to find articles about books, TV series, climate change, vaccines, cryptocurrencies, and…platforms!

Moving to *Business Insider*, a more tech-oriented outlet, the results are even wider. More than 20 results within the last 24 hours. News talks about Amazon, Facebook, and less known companies like Dolly, a tech-based last-mile delivery startup. Other articles talk about life-sciences companies, asset management, and cryptocurrencies or introduce Hubilo, a startup for virtual events.

Apple in 2010 registered a trademark for the claim "There's an app for that." Today we can probably say: "There's a platform for that!" And we can back it up with a little quick research on Crunchbase. The word "platform" is used in the description of 136,339 startups, while only 25,789 talk about "innovation," and 49,851 present themselves as "innovative."

The world platform is everywhere. Still, can people get it? Is it a meaningful word to people? Going back to the first tab we opened for this research, the Google one, we can easily find an answer. No. People do not clearly know what a platform is.

How can we say that? Well, we don't. Google does it for us. The search engine offers a nice view of what people search for, and the list is self-explaining:

- What do they mean by a platform?
- What is an example of a platform?
- What is the story of the platform?[2]
- What is a platform Wikipedia?
- Is Facebook a platform?
- How is a platform different from another?
- What are the different types of platforms?
- Is Microsoft Word a platform?

The message is one and only. What is a platform? Again, Google helps us. Just below the search bar, we can find its answer:

1: a level usually raised surface. We hurried to the train platform. 2: a raised floor or stage for performers or speakers. 3: a statement of the beliefs and rules of conduct for which a group stands. 4: an arrangement of computer components that uses a particular operating system.

The definition is a selected part, by the search engine, of a broader definition given by the Merriam Webster dictionary. Interesting, correct, and valuable. Still, is it in any way coherent with the news we got in the previous search? No, not at all.

---

[2] This is referring to "The Platform" a Netflix smash hit movie produced in Spain in 2019.

Google told us a lot! We know two things: first, the word "platform" is searched a lot; second, its meaning is not so clear. Let's follow one of the frequently asked questions and move to Wikipedia.

Things get clearer but even more complicated. The platform page on the English version of Wikipedia provides the following information.

Platform may refer to:

- *Technology*: computing platform, platform game, car platform, weapons platform, web platform, cryptocurrency exchange
- *Physical objects and features*: cargo platform, diving platform, oil platform, theater platform, platform shoe, railway platform, and so on
- *Politics*: party platform (a list of principles held by a political party), platform (an openly organized faction within a left-wing political party in the European politics), platformism (a form of anarchist organization that seeks unity from its participants)
- *Arts*: an art group, two movies (2000 by Jia Zhangke and 1993 Bollywood action movie), a novel, and a song by MIA
- *Others*: platform conodonts, a type of conodonts with highly evolved feeding elements, economic platform as an intermediary in a two-sided market, and a business model that creates value by facilitating exchanges between two or more interdependent groups

"Platform" is a popular word. "Platform" assumes different meanings in different environments. Therefore, we have no choice. Let's go back to the innovation management roots of platforms to find their original and evolving meaning.

The Roots: Product and Innovation Platforms

Product Platforms

To find the roots of platforms in the innovation management world, we need to forget about Facebook, Amazon, and Google and take a leap in time till the end of the 1970s. We also need to leave the United States, the recent homeland of many "platforms" that fill in news and examples, and reach the Far East. We stop in Japan.

The history of platforms for innovation has a significant milestone in the headquarters of Sony in 1979, when an iconic product was released: the Sony Walkman.

If you lived during those years, you certainly remember, and quite probably had, a Sony Walkman. If you are too young, please ask someone that was there or was a teenager till the 1990s. You'll surely see a smile popping up.

The Walkman was a revolutionary product. It enabled something that today is normal: to walk around listening to music. The original Walkman was a portable cassette player. Its popularity made "walkman" an unofficial term for portable cassette player of any producer or brand. Over the years, Sony has also used it for CD players and the first digital music players. By 2010, when production stopped, Sony had built about 200 million cassettes-based Walkmans.

The Walkman is a great business story, one of the greatest successes in Sony history. In the 1980s, Sony dominated a highly intensive competitive market, having 40 percent market share in units sold and almost 50 percent market share in value. This leadership was also remarkable because Sony was able to command a premium price of approximately U.S.$20.

Still, this is not why we present the Sony Walkman as a revolutionary case in the world of platforms.

During the 1980s, Sony launched more than 250 models of Walkman, far more than any competitor. One could expect this numerosity and leading market share position to drive to a sort of cannibalization: the new Walkman being sold at the expenses of the previous version. But, data collected by Sanderson and Uzumeri prove the contrary. The average obsolescence of Sony's portable cassette player (calculated as the time needed to have the product on the market at half of the launch price) was about 2 years, compared to 1.2 years for its competitors, meaning that Sony's products had a longer life cycle on the market. Part of the reason for this counterintuitive result is the variety of products targeting even narrow market niches. There was a Walkman for kids, one for classical music lovers, one super thin for tech addicts, even one to go underwater, and so on. The competition in these niches was lower while, on the main market, the abundance of competitors made it harsh.

Many products, many niches, slower obsolescence, higher premium price. How did Sony achieve these results and launch so many products in so few years? The answer lies in the leverage on a product platform strategy.

For 10 years, Sony launched and developed five generational projects, which laid the foundations for hundreds of products. There were three cassette player architectures: the WM2 launched in 1981, compact and lightweight, revised in 1990 to reduce its cost; the WMD launched in 1982, focused superior performances and hi-fi; and the WM20 launched in 1983 that was 50 percent thinner. Moreover, there were two-component innovations: the superflat motor in 1983, which was very thin and efficient in battery consumption, and the NiCd "chewing gum" battery developed in 1986.

Leveraging these five elements (three architectures and two components), Sony revolutionized the product development process, reducing the time and effort to develop the 250 products they launched.

It is interesting to note that none of these generational projects was a product itself. A basic architecture or the superflat motor was not a product and was not tradable on the market. They were basic elements (platforms) upon which to develop "derivative" products. The development process was relatively straightforward, first selecting one of the three basic architectures and then adding the components to derivate a functioning product. Many products shared both the architecture and some components being quite similar between them. Most of the development effort at this stage was not led by technical departments (crucial for the five generational projects) but by the marketing and sales to match the specific needs of a market niche.

From an innovation perspective, what they did was extremely interesting. Instead of starting from scratch every time, Sony invested heavily on three basic structures or platforms, which were the foundation on which they built all the subsequent models. These were long-term technology-intensive projects as they created the basis for products to be developed in 10 years. The development process was basically to derive a product from one of these platforms. This iterative and modular process

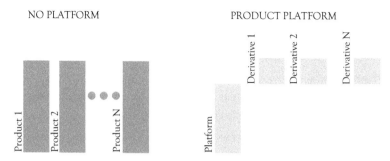

Figure 2.1 Product platforms

allowed the creation and launch of many new products with remarkable time and cost efficiency.

This example allows us to define a product platform (also known as internal platform back in the days) (Figure 2.1). A platform, according to Meyer and Lehnerd (1997), is a *set of components that create a basic structure common to many products.*

We can easily find another famous example of a product platform in the automotive industry. MQB is the platform developed by Volkswagen, which made it possible to simplify the design and production of many automotive models (even cross-brand like Seat, Volkswagen, Skoda, and Audi), to shorten the development process, and to make production plants more flexible based on the emerging market needs.

To better understand the concept of product platform, we can review some elements that can help us to identify the main advantages they unlock:

- A product platform allows to shorten the development time and reduce the cost of a new product by creating a basic architecture on which to develop multiple products called derivatives.
- A product platform offers advantages from a financial point of view. Huge investments are required for the platform that will then be paid back by a higher number of products launched on the market.
- A product platform makes the production process more flexible: even if a single model doesn't hit the market needs, other new models using the same platform can be easily developed to be successful.

At the same time, it is essential to note that the platform is not an actual product and, therefore, cannot be monetized directly. The platform becomes a tool through which the company can develop new products more efficiently.

It also entails a high risk: making a mistake on a platform means compromising a whole family of products for many years.

To sum it up, in this book, we are taking an innovation perspective on the role of platforms. We are aiming to understand how platforms can be a tool to foster innovation rather than just a business model to capture the value created. This goal, which may appear at least unconventional thinking about the "famous" platforms characterizing our days, is indeed highly coherent with this historical definition of platforms in the innovation management world: the product platform—a way (tightly coupled tool and business model) to increase the innovation performances of a company.

Innovation Platforms

Our journey continues in the 1980s, but moves to the United States. It is 1981, and Microsoft started to work on a program called "Interface Manager." It was the origin of the Windows project. This is the case milestone that drives us to the second type of platform: innovation platforms. We must talk about a product that changed the world: the personal computer designed by IBM in 1981 and the shift of the role of Microsoft and Intel from suppliers to platform leaders. The three companies combined their hardware and software components to create a central platform that replicated the typical dynamics of a product platform. It was a common starting point from which it was possible to derivate many products by leveraging existing components connected in basic architecture.

IBM created the architecture of the personal computer and, together with Microsoft and Intel, started selling it in the marketplace, convincing a range of consumers, starting from the business customers with spreadsheets and other killer apps. At the same time, Apple was developing a similar product targeting first the education market and later the creatives, artists, and musicians with a different approach, focusing on an integrated and controlled way of managing all the layers of its architecture and ensuring their coherent development.

It became suddenly clear that the computer was a product per se. Still, the primary source of value for the final customer was given by the functionalities enabled by applications built on top of the operating systems. For this reason, both Apple and Microsoft began to develop software applications to expand the computer's functionality; think, for example, of the word processors like Pages or Word.

Then, Microsoft took a decision that changed the world.

Unlike what Apple did, keeping the operating system closed and not allowing anyone to build applications on it, Microsoft decided to open the platform to external software developers allowing them to develop their products on top of the operating system. In this way, software producers like Lotus could offer their functionalities to the customers without developing the hardware (IBM and Intel) or the operating system (Microsoft) to make it work. All this was standard, open, and offered to anyone. Application developers (complementors) could concentrate 100 percent on developing software solutions that provide value to customers.

In this way, we see a part of the dynamics of the product platform replicated. Based on a set of pre-existing components, the hardware and the operating system, it is possible to develop new products without rebuilding the whole system from scratch.

The process of opening the platform was not limited to the involvement of the three players (IBM, Intel, and Microsoft) but expanded to allow other organizations to develop new applications for their architecture, further exploiting the potential of a platform.

This decision boosted the innovation process of thousands of companies opening a whole new prosperous industry based on software development. This is the reason why it is called an innovation platform.

But it also generated new value dynamics for the platform providers. Every time external companies decided to develop new software solutions on the platform created by IBM, Microsoft, and Intel, they increased the platform's value for the end customer. There are so many excellent software applications I need on the market. Hence, I must buy a Windows-based computer to use them.

This move induces two key features. First, this kind of platform generates a virtuous cycle of value creation and capture. The more developers choose to develop their services on a specific platform, the more end-users will choose that platform over competitors and vice versa, giving rise to the phenomenon of cross-side or indirect network externalities.

Second, the central platform created by IBM, Intel, and Microsoft became an intermediary between end-users and developers (often referred to as complementors), having other organizations creating value on their platform. Typically, the platform captures this value either by retaining a percentage of the transactions made between end-users and complementors or by charging complementors for accessing the platform. In other words, an innovation platform can capture value in two ways: first, by directly selling the platform, such as the computer; and second, allowing others to innovate on itself, and keeping part of the created value.

We can define, according to Gawer and Cusumano (2014), innovation platforms (Figure 2.2) as *products, services, or technologies that act as a foundation on which external innovators, called complementors, can develop their complementary products, services, or technologies, and offer them to users.*

Originally, innovation platforms were called "industry-wide platforms" because they have a role within the specific industry in which they operate and allow complementors to become part of the system. These external innovators can work on a semifinished product to have a basic structure supporting their work and reaching final customers. Besides the already mentioned computer created by IBM, Microsoft, and Intel, typical examples are all the operating systems, such as Android or iOS, that transformed smartphones from simple products into innovation platforms.

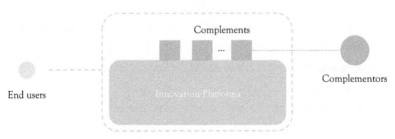

Figure 2.2 Innovation Platforms

Other examples are consoles for video games, which have on one side players and on the other side developers, but also open technological standards such as the DVD format.

Building a reference map for the concept of platform in the innovation world, we need to work also on the similarities and differences among the various types.

So, like product platforms, innovation platforms enable innovation by simplifying future development processes. Also, in this case, starting from a standard structure, we can get to very diversified and targeted products or services with lower development costs and time.

At the same time, differently from product platforms, an innovation platform is itself a product (e.g., like a game console). Companies can directly monetize the platform. It is also possible to capture value through innovations created by complementors. Obviously, we cannot overlook that opening to external actors will make this strategy less controllable than an internal platform, requiring the company or companies that create the platform to decide whether and how much to control and what third-party actors will be allowed to do or not on their platform.

To sum up, the platform concept has evolved, expanding in various directions, for example, leaving the perimeter of the single organization that characterized the idea of product platforms and involving other companies giving rise to the concept of innovation platform.

The Revolution: Platforms as an Innovative Business Model

Transactional Platforms

Let's continue our journey in the world of platforms. Let's reach 2008–2009 and stay in the United States, in the Silicon Valley. In those years, a couple of startups were fighting to emerge and would become enormous in a couple of years. Airbnb and Uber drive the list. They became the most famous and used examples of transactional platforms: platforms that enable a transaction between two parties, one searching and one offering something. These two companies lead a long list of digital companies that, in different fields, do something similar. They did not invent it. Booking. com and eBay were already doing something similar years before.

To introduce this new type of platform, we will use the most common and used example of it: credit cards. In this business, we have a focal actor at the center, such as MasterCard or Visa, which connects two different types of actors: the people who own a credit card, which we will call first side; and the merchants who accept that credit card as a payment method, which we will call second side.

A credit card is a tool that connects someone looking for something to someone offering it, in this case facilitating the economic transaction even in the absence of cash, making the transaction smoother, easier, and safer. The original business model is very simple: the service is practically free for the first side, while a percentage of the transaction is withheld from the merchant, who pays for both groups' service. Today, more complex combinations depend on the specific credit card, but one side is still fully or partially subsidized by the other.

Typically, platforms like credit cards bring together a demand side—a group of people looking for a good or service—with a supply side, a group offering that service. One could look at it with a customer–supplier relationship between the two sides or, otherwise, taking the perspective of the central platform, one could see both as customers. Mastercard or Visa offers a service to both cardholders and merchants, giving them the ability to use and accept this payment method.

This is the first key feature of transactional platforms (Figure 2.3): two groups of customers are directly linked together. In fact, the service offering is tied precisely to creating a link between the two sides.

The second defining characteristic is related to the platform value. The credit card itself has no value to those who own it unless merchants are ready to accept it. At the same time, the value perceived by the merchants in taking that credit card will increase with the number of card owners who can be perceived as a potential market.

This mechanism derives from network effects.[3] and is called indirect or cross-side network externalities. The value of these platforms is defined

---

[3] Network effect (or network externality) is the phenomenon by which part of the value or utility a user derives from a good or service depends on the number of users of compatible products. For a more in-depth analysis of network goods and their value generation dynamics, please refer to Chapter 5.

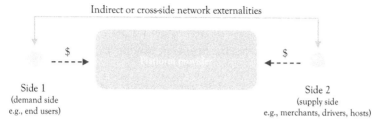

Figure 2.3 Transactional platforms

based on the cross-side numerosity of the actors on the two sides. In other words, the system has no intrinsic value unless there are many actors on one side, which creates value for users on the other side. Having two sets of customers interconnected by cross-side externalities means that this kind of platform is very different from traditional businesses. In a traditional business, the company has suppliers and customers and creates value by transforming inputs into an output, which we can call linear value chain businesses.

These two characteristics (having two distinct customers and the existence of cross-side externalities) mean that launching a business of this kind involves different difficulties.

Every traditional company has the problem of convincing customers of the value of its innovation. But since the value of our idea depends on how many users we have on the opposite side (and at the beginning we don't have any), we must convince customers of an idea that has no measurable value yet. In this case, however, we must convince two groups of customers of the value of our idea.

That's why we talk about the chicken-and-egg paradox: it's very difficult to convince people to own a credit card that no merchant accepts yet. At the same time, it's very difficult to convince merchants to accept a credit card if nobody owns it.

The possibility of offering the service free of charge to a side, as mentioned earlier, often helps to get out of this paradox, choosing to subsidize the side that is most price sensitive and therefore difficult to convince.

Linked directly to this first difficulty is a second one: the definition of the pricing strategy. How can we define the price of a service if its value depends on the number of players who will participate in the system?

This is the dilemma that has interested the researchers who first studied this kind of business. The answer lies in the value of the cross-price elasticity of demand between the two sides, making it possible to identify the best side to subsidize.

The original concept behind credit cards is that of the two-sided market by Rochet and Tirole (2003). For years, researchers considered having two distinct customers and leveraging cross-side externalities as something intrinsic to some specific markets, such as credit cards. Over time, however, we have realized that this is not an inherent feature of a market but rather a clear innovation choice by the organization creating the platform.

If you think of some of the most successful companies born in the new millennium, it is easy to see how many leverage this very business model. We can refer to the previously mentioned Airbnb, Uber, Booking.com, or the older eBay, but also Spotify, the Amazon Marketplace, Deliveroo, Glovo, and so on. We deal with organizations whose primary objective is to create a basic platform that allows different groups of players to get in touch, get to know each other, and establish a transaction. The two-sided market model then evolves into the so-called transactional two-sided platform or, more simply, transactional platforms (see Trabucchi and Buganza 2022).

This basic structure allows you to create value not by offering a product or a service but by connecting different groups of customers you are looking for.

A transactional platform can be defined as products or services where two or multiple groups of customers get together through a platform that profits from internalizing indirect network externalities. What these platforms do is to sell transactions to both parties, to enable a proper matchmaking.

Again, we can draw parallels regarding the other types of platforms: like product platforms, we have a central body, without intrinsic value, that enables value creation. At the same time, unlike a product platform, the basic platform does not allow the generation of new products but only enables transactions between the sides.

Like innovation platforms, we have two, or potentially more, customer groups involved that generate cross-network externalities. Different from innovation platforms, however, the platform cannot exist without having both sides on board, making the launch of a two-sided transactional platform much more complex. This last characteristic clearly differentiates innovation and transactional platforms, which otherwise may be confused due to cross-side externalities. A tip to keep in mind the difference: iOS is an innovation platform, since it enables developers to create something new that will enhance the iPhone, while the Apple App Store is a transactional platform that lets end-users get in touch with developers.

Orthogonal Platforms

The easy job is done. We introduced the three "most famous" types of platforms in the innovation management world. Still, we haven't finished. At the beginning of the chapter, we reported the frequently asked questions on Google regarding the term "platform." One of them was: "Is Facebook a platform?" Similarly, in the early days of our work on platforms, we found a paper titled "Is the Google platform a two-sided market?" by Luchetta (2014). Two similar questions, with different assumptions. Is Google a platform? Why? How? Is it Facebook? Are they two-sided markets? Does this mean they are transactional platforms? Well, no. So, what are they?

The short answer is yes, both are platforms, but a particular kind of platform we haven't discussed yet: orthogonal platforms. The long answer is a bit more complicated than that and brings us back to our time machine. New continent, Europe, different century: it is 1836, the foundation year of La Press, one of the historical French newspapers.

This French newspaper was the first to include paid advertising in its pages, lowering its price, extending its readership, and increasing its profitability. Obviously, the formula was soon copied by all titles.

Around 1840, Volney Palmer established the roots of the modern-day advertising agency in Philadelphia. In 1842, Palmer bought large amounts of space in various newspapers at a discounted rate, then resold the space at higher rates to advertisers. The actual advertisement—the copy, layout, and artwork—was still prepared by the company wishing to advertise; in effect, Palmer was just a space broker. The situation changed when the first full-service advertising agency of N. W. Ayer & Son was founded in 1869 in Philadelphia. Ayer & Son offered to plan, create, and execute complete advertising campaigns for its customers. By 1900, the advertising agency had become the focal point of creative planning, and advertising was firmly established as a profession.

Trying to model what we have seen in this historical excursus: newspapers have a publisher who coordinates a series of activities that flow into a daily publication distributed through a complex logistical system. The final newspaper is sold at a modest price; it only partially covers the production and distribution costs. This is made possible by the fact that another player subsidizes readers in the marketplace: advertisers.

The advertisers always interact with the publisher, but to buy a very different service from the information offered by the newspaper, they buy the readers' eyeballs.

We find ourselves in a typical two-sided mechanism, with a central actor that builds the platform—the publisher—going to sell two complementary services to two different groups of customers: the reader and the brands that pay for the advertising space.

However, let's immediately highlight the first significant difference with two-sided transactional platforms: the platform does not enable any transaction between the two sides. In other words, the newspaper does not allow its readers to buy the product seen in the advertisement; it simply exposes them to its existence—even if they are not interested in it.

We have two sides, but a transaction between them is not enabled, so in the graphical representation, we move the second side away from the transaction line, moving it orthogonally with respect to the transaction space with the first side. Therefore, we talk about orthogonal or nontransactional two-sided platforms (Figure 2.4), differentiating them from the more classic cases such as credit cards or Uber that enable a transaction instead. This is a widespread mechanism and not even particularly innovative. All the services based on advertising work precisely in this way, and Google is a crystal-clear example.

To be more even precise, the case of Google perfectly represents an orthogonal platform leveraging a strategy called client-as-a-target; in other words, the platform uses the first side as a target for the second.

The differences with transactional structures, however, are not limited to this. In fact, the first side receives a service that depends solely on the

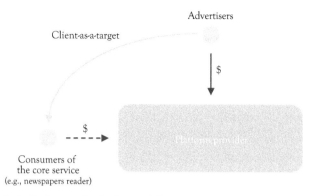

Figure 2.4 Orthogonal platforms (client-as-a-target)

central platform. Basically, we are dealing with a business that has all the characteristics of a linear value chain. Google's operations to offer a search engine as well as a newspaper's processes to deliver the next issue do not need any advertiser to happen. This is not true in the case of transactional platforms like Airbnb: without the hosts and their houses, the platform could not offer any service to the guests. In orthogonal two-sided platforms, the second side becomes an opportunity to make the business model economically sustainable by capturing the value created, but does not participate in the value creation process for the first side.

Therefore, we can define orthogonal platforms as products or services based on the sale of two different services to two different groups of customers who do not directly contact each other. These platforms rely on a unidirectional cross-side network externality. In this case, the value for advertisers increases as the number of readers of the newspaper increases, but the reverse is not valid.

In particular, the client-as-a-target strategy uses the first side as an asset to be exploited by offering its attention to the second side. The latter is involved in making the platform's business model sustainable or more sustainable, paying not only for the service received but also for the service provided in the first side.

It may be interesting to see how the client-as-a-target strategy can be used also within a transactional two-sided platform. For example, Booking .com enables hotel owners to pay for sponsored listing and appear on top of the results when someone searches for the location they are in.

This takes the name of supply-side advertising and is the same strategy; the platform—on top of transactions—is also selling eyeballs, but done with two transactional players, but taking place within the ecosystems of players that were already there for different reasons.

In our journey to define various types of platforms, we have talked about many big techs that have changed the lives of millions of people since the second decade of the 2000s. Until now, however, we never used social networks as examples. This might be surprising as, in the common language, they are among the typical examples of platforms. Now we will analyze one of the most famous social networks in the world, Twitter, which—and it's no coincidence that we underline this in the opening—is also a totally free service for the end-user.

Twitter is the social network that allows you to write short messages (tweets) and share them with the world. Here, it is important to point out that, unlike Facebook or other social networks, Twitter relies on the idea of hashtags that allow content to travel around the social network independently of one's circle of contacts, potentially reaching all people interested in that topic.

Advertisers on the platform pay to promote specific tweets, hashtags, or profiles, making Twitter an orthogonal platform that uses a client-as-a-target strategy—but there's much more than that.

Twitter, unlike newspapers, collects a variety of data during service delivery that can be used in many ways. For example, during the 2012 U.S. presidential campaign, Twitter realized that a great value was hidden in their tweets and created the Twitter Political Index: an index to show trends in sentiment toward Obama and Romney. The idea was simple: by counting the number of tweets mentioning Obama (or Romney) and measuring "the mood (or sentiment)" of the tweets by looking at the presence of positive (or negative) words in the same tweets, the index could measure the pulse of the (Twitter) nation toward the candidates.

Based on the analysis of sentiments expressed in tweets related to the two contenders, this index opened new scenarios for market research.

Shortly after, Twitter created a new service that allows companies to directly purchase packages of tweets related to a specific topic to enable a series of analyses and allow this new client to know what the Twitter population thinks about a given topic. Customers of this service can be any research-related firm interested in understanding what the world thinks, instantaneously, on a given topic. This service may not be mainstream, but looking at Twitter's financial documents, we can see how the voice "Data licensing and other" in the 2020 financial report accounts for 13.6 percent of the overall revenues of the platform.

Let's read this example based on the orthogonal two-sided platform model. We face a platform with a new orthogonal set of customers who are offered data collected during the basic service delivered to the first side. Unlike before, however, the logic behind the value creation mechanism is the opposite. The orthogonal side leverages the mass of Twitter users as a source of data rather than a target for advertisement, moving from a client-as-a-target logic to a client-as-a-source logic. These transactions must comply with privacy regulations, but do not invalidate the value of this logic. The value of the data collected depends on their numerosity, and the orthogonal client is interested in aggregate data and trends, not in the data of the individual client.[4]

Let us also highlight here how, in the example of Twitter, we were talking about data that are meant to be shared with the world, being tweets public for the purpose of the service itself.

In conclusion, it is worth noting how, with this orthogonal logic, two-sided platforms become an opportunity to make innovation by broadening the business model and increasing the portion of value captured by the platform.

To conclude, we want to stress that orthogonal platforms leveraging a client-as-a-source strategy (Figure 2.5) rely on unidirectional cross-side network externalities (as it was for those leveraging a client-as-a-target strategy).

Market researchers are interested in how many tweeters provide data, while the number of market researchers is not interesting for the users who enjoy the platforms.

Just as in the case of client-as-a-target, this platform strategy is very often the second evolutionary step for these companies. They started with linear logic and found in the platform business model a way to capture

---

[4] Chapter 4 will focus on orthogonal platforms, define various strategies, and go in-depth into the various data-related scandals and privacy-related concerns.

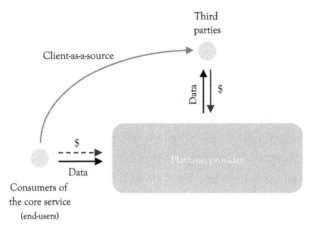

Figure 2.5 **Orthogonal platforms (client-as-a-source)**

the value created by the final customers to pay any money for the service they receive.

It's worth noting, however, that all orthogonal logics (client-as-a-source strategy and client-as-a-target) are close to other forms of platforms—like innovation or transactional platforms—since the demand side directly creates value that the platform can capture—by bringing a second side on board.

Hybrid Platforms

The journey was long, various centuries, different continents, and four types of platforms. A recap is needed.

Platform in the innovation world is a misleading word; we should use at least four different "labels" to make sense of what we mean:

- Product platforms are sets of components and technologies that generate a basic architecture on which multiple products can be developed, reducing the new product development time and cost, as in the case of Sony Walkman.
- Innovation platforms open the idea of product platforms to the market, allowing anyone to develop products on top of a basic platform, as in the case of computers with their operating systems and external software developers. The

platform is itself a product, and the concept of network
externalities emerges here.

- Transactional platforms take us into the world of two-sided
  platforms, enabling the transaction between two groups of
  users offering and seeking something, as in the case of Airbnb.
  Indirect or cross-side network externalities remain, as in
  innovation platforms, but as in product platforms, the
  platform has no extrinsic value.

- Two-sided platforms can also be orthogonal when the second
  side, figuratively, moves away from the transaction line. The
  network externalities become unilateral: more users represent a
  greater value for advertisers, but the opposite is not true. Here we
  have two possible strategies. First, we have the client-as-a-target
  logic, where the first side is the target of an advertising message
  by the orthogonal side, as in the case of Google. Second, we have
  the client-as-a-source logic where the mechanism is enabled by
  data generated by the first side, as in the case of Twitter, and the
  platform sells data to third parties interested in market research
  and trends. Unlike the previous platforms, orthogonal platforms
  rely on a linear value chain, and the second (orthogonal) side is
  involved only to capture the value created.

Platforms were born as a way (tightly coupled tool and business
model) to make the process of new product development—and therefore
innovation—more effective and efficient (product platforms).

The innovation platforms follow soon and meet, before its formal definition, the spirit of open innovation by opening to the outside world. We
then reach the two- and multisided world with transactional and orthogonal platforms. Here we meet those companies like Uber or Facebook,
which made the concept of platform universally known in the 2000s but
also seem more distant from the initial usage of platform strategies as
enablers for innovation.

Having clearly in mind these four typologies of platforms is a key first
step to becoming a platform thinker. Consider that, even if they seem to
be complex and variegated, they are just single "words" in the language
of platforms. These words can then be mixed and added to build phrases

that capture the real complexity of what we see every day but might fail to understand fully.

What do we mean?

Well, Apple speaks this language perfectly, showing us that we need many of these words to really describe what they do.

When defining transactional platforms, we used Apple as an emblematic case to distinguish innovation and transactional platforms. iOS (with its technological components of iPhones, its technological architecture, and its APIs[5] for external developers) is a typical example of an innovation platform, while the App Store is a typical example of a two-sided transactional platform with the sole purpose of enabling transactions between those who search and those who offer applications.

But it doesn't end here. Apple is famous for many things, from impeccable product design to high service levels, not to mention the innovative scope of many of its products. But there is something more that characterizes it: the product families, where we can easily find excellent examples of product platforms. The iPhone architecture allowed the development, on an annual basis, of one or more iPhone models as derivative products, maintaining—at least for some generations of smartphones—the same basic architecture and making the development process shorter and more effective (Figure 2.6).

This simple example shows us how companies can integrate all types of platforms into a single organization creating hybrid platforms—and that the world of platforms is much more complicated than it might seem.

The iPhone is a
product
platform

iOS is an
innovation
platform

The App Store is a
transactional
platform

Figure 2.6 Apple as a hybrid platform

---

[5] An application programming interface (API) is a way for two or more computer programs to communicate with each other. It is a type of software interface, offering a service to other pieces of software.

Reframing

Does it make sense to talk about innovation when talking about platforms?

We mentioned various cases, like Airbnb and Uber, as the flagship cases of this platform revolution, but we can also find slightly older cases in the club of big platforms. Companies like Booking.com, eBay, PayPal, or even Amazon were born between the second half of the 1990s and the first part of the new millennium. Nevertheless, the basic model behind these companies looks back to the idea of market and to old cases like the credit cards. Why does such a classic model become the emblem of innovation in the new millennium?

The answer is straightforward and lies in the digital technologies, which can make a model as old as the market, efficient, and highly scalable, as it never was before.

Let's consider the two dynamics together: the spread of digital technologies on the one side and the platform revolution on another. We can easily see that their cojoint action is opening the way to a shiny era of innovation.

Let us show this with a simple example about Uber. In 2015, Aswath Damoradan, a professor at New York University, launched a debate about the company's valuation. In those months, private investors had participated in funding rounds of 1.2 billion dollars, suggesting a value of the company of 17 billion dollars.[6]

The professor described this value as "a mind-boggling sum," a figure that was simply absurd given that the company in question had positive results but was still small in terms of market penetration and revenues.

The debate was taken up by Bill Gurley, a partner at Benchmark Capital, one of Uber's main investors. He publicly stated that yes, the valuation made by the market, as claimed by Damoradan, was wrong. But unlike the professor's claim, Gurley argued that the evaluation was underestimating the company's actual value, as it lacked consideration of

---

[6] For a wider analysis, please refer to G.G. Parker, M.W. Van Alstyne, and S.P. Choudary. 2016. *Platform Revolution: How Networked Markets Are Transforming the Economy and How to Make Them Work for You* (Boston: WW Norton and Company).

the potential market and network effects underlying the entire system. Within a few years, without going public, Uber's value would exceed tens of billions of dollars, reaching as high as $60 to $70 billion at times.

This short story makes us understand the innovative potential we're talking about: a company like Uber is so far from the traditional logic of value creation and capturing to put even the most established finance tools for the valuation of a company in crisis.

We could make similar examples using other classic models in the world of management, such as Porter's value chain, which involves a transfer of value from suppliers to the company, that, through internal operations, creates additional value to be then proposed to the market, or Christensen's disruptive innovation that argues the need of a niche market interested in investing in low-performing products to make them slowly grow up to the point they are interesting for the mass market.

However, in the world of platforms, we do not find this linearity or this time dynamics anymore. On the contrary, we see a much more complex system where the company acts as an orchestrator of value, serving different customers and disrupting industries in a few years, if not months.

In other words, we are saying that the platform model is not innovative per se. Still, its cojoint effect with the digital revolution is shaking the foundations of almost all the industries we know. This calls for major innovation in the management world, generating new frameworks, strategies, tools, and models—and a new mindset.

Platforms are already promising new business models that undermine customers' traditional ideas for what they receive. We are so accustomed to free services like social networks that we start asking why we must pay for other services like newspapers. All industries will have to cope with this soon.

Let's consider, for example, what Spotify did to the music industry, enabling the transition from music ownership to access to a music library, disrupting not only the fruition of music by the end-user but also the commercial logic with which music is created, promoted, and brought to the market.

The innovative power of platforms, though, goes beyond the same platforms. We are accustomed to talking about digital startup platforms, but their effect already shakes old, traditional businesses.

This example shows how the platform revolution can help in fostering innovation even in existing and established businesses.

To conclude: no, platforms are not an innovation per se. We are talking about an ancient concept, but one that digital technologies have been able to bring to its full splendor, making it a true innovation enabler—an enabler that requires the skillful and careful eye of the innovator to see in this ancient tool the possibility of doing something new and changing the way we are used to operating in our sector.

Hence, the need to switch to "platform thinking," the ability to use platform-based mechanisms to unlock digital business transformations, the chance to see platforms where they are not and to consider them an effective way of orchestrating resources to unveil new and relevant opportunities for innovation. For this reason, we briefly introduce the reference framework of the book that will be explored throughout the next chapters.

We will consider the platform having two sets of sides—transactional and orthogonal—that enable three different sets of strategies (Figure 2.7):

- Transactions: The two sides join the platform in order to meet one another.
- Client-as-a-target: The orthogonal side joins the platform to get to the "eyeballs" of the first side.
- Client-as-a-source: The orthogonal side joins the platform to exploit the data generated by the first side.

These three strategies populate the multisided space of platforms that will be explored in the next two chapters.

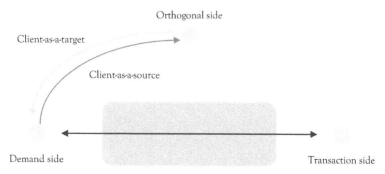

Figure 2.7 The reference framework

Platform Thinking World: The MOOC "What's Beyond Uber?"

This chapter lives also as an entire course we developed, produced by METID Politecnico di Milano, and available on Coursera; check it out: "Platform Thinking: What's Beyond Uber?" (Figure 2.8).

Figure 2.8 QR code for the platform thinking MOOC "What's Beyond Uber?"

Source: bit.ly/PT_MOOC1.

CHAPTER 3

How to Design a Platform

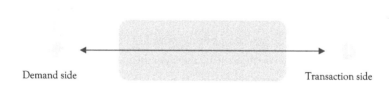

Demand side   Transaction side

Design the Platform Value Drivers

We saw the historical evolution of platforms, from product platforms to various kinds of two- or multisided platforms. Keeping in mind also the original definitions of product and innovation platforms, which will be very useful in the last part of the book, we will now focus on transactional and orthogonal platforms and, more broadly, on two- or multisided platforms. We are referring to all those cases that gained huge prominence over the second decade of the new millennium, from Airbnb to Uber, from Spotify to Deliveroo, and so on.

First, we need to understand what they really do. Connecting those who are looking for a product or a service with those who can offer it is certainly the most evident activity, but building a platform goes far beyond this. To become platform thinkers, we need to understand the real essence of what these companies do and explore how they create value.

Matchmaking...Is It Just That?

Taking a user perspective, and thinking back to the taxi driver's case that opened the book, it may seem that these platforms "do nothing." They "just matchmake someone that searches with someone that offers something." This idea generated hundreds of "wannabe platforms" that created a website to match people on the market. But the reality is that most of them failed miserably and made it quite clear: The only reason it seems they "do nothing" is because they can manage a high degree of complexity and deliver easy-to-use services to the final customers.

Platforms are indeed complex organizations. The great job of platforms is done behind the scenes. Platform providers need to spend an enormous amount of time and effort to actively design and continuously improve the platform itself. Platforms do many activities to create value for all the parties involved in the system and to make sure that everyone has a share of this value.

The fact that platforms "do nothing" and just "matchmake" is a false myth. This chapter is all about this, the dynamics, and peculiarities that platform providers—and therefore, also platform thinkers—need to consider to properly design and evolve a platform.

Let's dig into this by going back to the end of the 1990s and reading the words of Evans and Schmalensee:

> It's Saturday morning in the summer of 1998. Julie Templeton's mom and dad are coming into town the next weekend. She and her husband, Chuck, want to treat them to a gala restaurant weekend in San Francisco, with dinners out Friday, Saturday, and Sunday nights.
>
> Julie starts dialing for reservations. No answer. She leaves a message. She keeps calling, restaurant after restaurant. Some don't have anything on the evenings she wants. One she wants to go to on Sunday isn't open. Almost four hours later, after a lot of calling and juggling, she's got the weekend planned.
>
> Back then, making dinner reservations was hard. Taking them was, also. Most restaurants still took reservations over the phone. Someone wrote them down with a pencil, on paper, in a notebook. Often, tables went empty if the phone didn't ring enough. Restaurants had no way to let people know when they had tables available.

Julie Templeton's persistence paid off. Most people, though, just aren't willing to work that hard to get a restaurant reservation. As a result, in 1998, on a typical Saturday night in San Francisco, there were unhappy couples sitting at home, perhaps having take-out pizza, who had given up trying to get a table for their date night, and unhappy restaurant owners with tables sitting empty, not making ends meet in a tough business.

The market for matching up diners with tables at restaurants wasn't working very well. Restaurants and diners spent a lot of resources—time and effort—getting together, and even so tables went empty, and diners stayed home. That's the sort of problem that an important, but until recently overlooked, type of business sets out to solve by helping parties who have something valuable to exchange find each other, get together, and do a deal.

With these words, Evans and Schmalensee—in their book *Matchmakers*—tell the genesis of one of the most famous platforms born in the late 1990s: Open Table.

During the following year, 1999, Julie and her husband Chuck Templeton decided to put an end—or at least give an alternative—to what happened the previous summer. It doesn't make sense for people to spend time looking for a restaurant that is waiting to be called … while the restaurateur is hoping to be called. Identifying this friction—the fact that two economic players are looking for each other and struggling—is the starting point for the creation of Open Table.

The promise is simple: to help people make restaurant reservations and to help restaurants fill empty tables as well.

The initial solution was a website that would allow people to search for and book a restaurant, totally free of charge for the final users. It was the dawn of the new millennium, and finding funding for a website was easy—even though the dot.com bubble would soon burst.

Convincing restaurants was more complex, for various reasons: Many did not have computers, and it was difficult to convince them to pay for an untested service. Julie and Chuck understood they had to do more to bring restaurants on board. They identified a major pain that many restaurants shared: the lack of a proper table management system. So, they developed one and offered a way to help restaurants go beyond the paper and pencil reservation management. The reservation system was provided for an installation fee and a monthly rental fee. Initially, they focused on a few cities like San Francisco, Chicago, New York, and Washington. Despite their initial success, by the end of 2001, they were close to bankruptcy and needed a major refund. After recovering, they went public in 2009 with a market cap on day 1 of $626 million and finally sold the platforms to Priceline in 2014 for $2.6 billion.

This brief and simple story brings up several key points about the world of platforms:

- You don't need particularly brilliant or complex ideas to create a platform; the everyday problem such as booking a restaurant that inspired Julie and Chuck makes that clear.

- The first solution may be very simple, like the website to match diners and restaurants, but its adoption for one or more sides might be unpaired by internal operational and hidden problems that need to be identified and solved to make the "simple" solution suitable. Open Table is much more than the matchmaking website. The table management system is not a nice add-on; it is the cornerstone of the system, hidden from the final users' eyes.

- It seems simple to identify the needs of both customers— people who are looking for the restaurant and restaurateurs who don't want empty tables—everything is very rational, but convincing both to get on the platform is anything but simple.

- Often, on platforms not all players pay. In this case, only restaurants pay for the service, while end-users enjoy it for free.

- Within a few years, the valuation had reached very high figures, but the growth was not linear and had many bumps, even filing for bankruptcy.

These observations allow us to clearly define the playing field on which platforms are created and grown.

1. Transactional platforms aim to *reduce transaction costs* (see Williamson 1979), so the identification of the two sides—and therefore the two sets of customers—and of a first value proposition, linked to the transaction itself, is very simple, reinforcing the false myth that "they do almost nothing."

2. The value of the platform depends on *cross-side network externalities*: The value perceived by the end customers depends on the quantity of actors operating on the other side, in this case the restaurateurs, and, in the same way, the value for restaurants to use the platform increases with the number of users.

3. Unfortunately, this mechanism works extremely well once you have enough actors on both sides (enough customers using the service and enough restaurants to be booked on the other side). The main and major problem is how to start from scratch and manage the *ramp-up phase*, how to get to that *critical mass* (on both sides) that allows the system to run smoothly and autonomously instead of asking the restaurateurs to pay for their act of faith in the value that one day the platform will bring them.

4. The idea of reducing the transaction cost is extremely valuable but not enough to convince both sides to get on board. Just after having identified the market friction, the platform thinker must stop looking at the problem as one. There are *two different customers and therefore two value propositions* are needed. The real needs and constraints of each side must be carefully addressed to develop meaningful value promises able to satisfy their individual needs and, at the same time, be complementary in supporting them. This implies acquiring some knowledge about the linear value chains of the sides to find how to solve their internal constraints to platform adoption, as in the case of the table management system that was developed to give more value to the most reluctant restaurateurs.

5. Once the *ramp-up phase is over*, network externalities rapidly lead to the scalability of the platform, justifying its ability to attract huge funds.

The cross-externalities are at the core of platforms. They are the reason why platforms have been able, in some cases, to gather a particularly high level of investors' attention around them and, on the strength of their ability, to scale in a very short time by rapidly opening dozens of markets and gathering millions of users.

In the case of digital platforms, often (but not always),[1] there is a second element that boosts the scalability even more: a structure based on zero marginal costs (Rifkin 2014). In these cases, having a new customer does not increase costs because the platform simply needs to create a direct link between customers who are on two different sides. In other words, having a new restaurant or end-user for Open Table does not result in higher costs, only more revenue in the case of the restaurateur.

Nevertheless, this situation is only achievable if the cross-network externalities are in place and the ramp-up period is over.

In the end, transactional platforms might appear as simple matchmakers, smart people who found a market friction and made a lot of money out of it. There is much more than that. This limited understanding of what a platform is and what it does is the reason why hundreds of wannabe platforms have failed and still fail in their attempt. To become a platform thinker, we must look behind the matchmaking visible in the front-end and fully understand to what extent platforms are different from linear value chain organizations and what are their value drivers, constraints, and opportunities. Said another way, a platform thinker must deeply know how platforms create value.

...No, Platforms Do Create Value

To explore the value drivers that characterize the platforms' work, we continue our journey through time and space. Let's go back a few years. It's December 2003; Fred Mazzella was trying to go to his hometown in the Vendée region in the west of France to spend Christmas with his family. All trains were fully booked during the busy period, and no seats

---

[1] Not all the digital platforms are based on a zero-marginal cost structure. In the case of Spotify, for example, more customers or more customer usage of the platform, force the company to pay more money for music rights to the artists.

were available until after Christmas. Eventually, he managed to convince his sister to pick him up from Paris, a major detour for the sibling who lived in Normandy. As he was driving with her on the highway, he saw a train that he wanted to take. It was indeed overbooked, with all seats occupied. At the same time, whizzing past his car were hundreds of cars that were mostly empty except for the drivers. It was a eureka moment! In 2006, Fred purchased the domain name Covoiturage.fr (French for "car sharing") and, along with Nicolas and Francis, founded a company called Camuto that would soon become BlaBlaCar, a platform that connects drivers and passengers and helps them share the costs of journeys.

A few years later, it is April 24, 2018; we are still in France. Besides being the founder of the company, Fred still acts as a driver to listen to the customers, and that day he meets a kind of surprising customer. Trains are on strike, and Fred takes on board a retired couple who were using the service for the first time. The couple complained a bit about the difficulties they encountered when signing up on the platform. The system required a Facebook account to sign up, and it took them a while to create one and complete all the formalities. Still, they were there enjoying the ride and delighted to be on their way toward their grandchildren's birthday party (for more details, see Saxena et al. 2020).

This brief history gives us some elements to reflect on.

Despite not being hassle-free, the sign-up mechanism achieved the unthinkable. If we go back to the mid-2000s, when Fred created the platform, it would have been hard to imagine that a few years later, elderly people would be using BlaBlaCar to get around. Why? Let's say meeting someone via a smartphone and accepting a ride in exchange for digital money withdrawn from a credit card could have been a great description for a horror movie for aged people. The limit to diffusion was a lack of trust in the technology, in the people, and in online digital payments. But distrust was not only on the customers' side. Drivers were also scared of bringing onboard unknown people who could be dangerous for their belongings or even their lives.

This is the most important element that emerges from this story: The trust problem was probably the biggest they had to face, and they solved it so brilliantly that even that segment of the population they would have never dared to target became their customers.

They achieved this result by requiring the verification of Facebook profiles to show a face to the passengers, but they also added the request for specific information on the driver's license, the feedback about passengers by previous drivers, and the management of the money transfer (released only at the end of the ride). They implemented a series of small actions to generate trust from both sides of customers toward the platform, but most of all between them.

They worked so hard on it that they created a proprietary framework, called DREAMS, to indicate all the elements built into the platform to manage trust.

In other words, the platform worked hard to create value, generating and enabling trust in the system, despite those who believe that a platform does nothing and that, after identifying the friction to be solved, everything comes by itself.

Designing platforms requires a particularly complex value proposition effort. The platform must offer a value proposition for both sides. You need to design a value proposition for both the first and second sides, knowing that creating a link between them will only be a solid starting point. You need to figure out why they want to use the platform and also why they might decide not to.

The platform provider's job goes far beyond matching the two sides and encompasses other value drivers that a successful platform should leverage (see Trabucchi et al. 2021b).

We dedicated a lot of space to the mechanisms of trust-building, with the BlaBlaCar example, because it is often a key enabler of transactions. Still, we need to remember that drivers typically used in digital services—even if they are not necessarily platforms—remain extremely valuable in the platform world, possibly slightly revised. One of them is, for example, related to the creation of a *feeling of community*; in this way, the platform tries to increase the frequency of interaction with customers to feed the network externalities that exist between the two sides and ensure a good number of customers on both sides. An example of this is offered by Airbnb, which often organizes gatherings of hosts with the aim of making them feel like part of a large community. Another example is related to perceived personalization. It is important to ensure that the quality of possible matches between the two sides is so high to prove a sense of *personalization* in the matchmaking. Think, for example, to Amazon, and the customized suggestions based on prior experience on the platform, or even more Netflix or Spotify that offer a unique homepage given the previous movies watched or songs listened to.

Design the Platform Launch (and the Early Stages)

The launch of a platform is probably the most difficult phase. We already said that network cross-externalities would work and be effective once they reached the critical mass (number of customers) on both sides. Going rapidly and efficiently through this early stage is vital, and here we want to focus on strategies and approaches to make it happen. First we will review how to approach the chicken-and-egg paradox, then we will focus on whom and how to charge to create revenues, then we will see the power of including in the ecosystem some enhancers (stakeholders interested in supporting the platform growth), and finally we will analyze the quantity or quality dilemma (if it is wiser to add as many customers as possible on both sides or carefully select those who provide more quality to the system).

Approaching the Chicken-and-Egg Paradox

The early days of platforms were tough. To prove the value of a new product is difficult; to prove that of a platform is even harder. To understand why, we move to Italy, back in 2014, and we meet Alessandro.

Alessandro Cadoni is a young Italian management engineering student with a great passion for social networks.

He is particularly attracted by the work of influencers, people who get paid by brands to use their followings on social networks such as Facebook or Instagram to promote their products or services. Nothing particularly innovative, it's just a new way of being a testimonial for a brand.

Alessandro, however, asks himself a very simple question. Why, instead of a few influencers being followed by millions of people they really don't know, can't we change the perspective toward hundreds of thousands of normal people, turning them into "small size" influencers followed by people who really know and trust them personally? From this simple intuition, Friendz was born (for the whole story, see Trabucchi and Buganza 2021).

Friendz is a groundbreaking startup involved in digital marketing. Their goal is to stimulate web users into promoting brands they love through their active participation in creative campaigns tailored purposely for each company.

The users' interest in participating in the campaigns is stimulated by the reward they can gain, consisting of virtual credits they can spend on e-commerce; the philosophy is that users are known directly by their friends and are mainly supporting campaigns for brands they really love. The aim of the reward is only to encourage users to take and publish high-quality pictures when these are associated with the brand. Moreover, the users' contents are verified and approved by the staff before being published and made visible to other people, so that the company has a further guarantee concerning the quality of the images.

This is what Friendz does, but let's go back to the beginning of the story: Alessandro, a young student, an idea, and nothing else. How can you launch such an idea on the market? You can start by convincing people who will take and post the photos to subscribe to the service. Unfortunately, though, without brands offering the campaigns, it would not make sense for them to sign up. You could try to convince a brand to buy this new marketing service. But again, who would buy it without having users on the other side and examples of what they can do?

This situation clearly illustrates a paradox: You need both sides to get the platform going, but one without the other is not motivated to get on. Where do we start? What comes first?

This phenomenon is known as the chicken-and-egg paradox and characterizes all transactional, two-sided platforms. We could recount the same paradox in the launch of a new credit card or in the creation of Airbnb or Uber. How does one resolve this situation?

In literature, Evans and Schmalensee highlight three strategies to address this paradox: zigzag, two-steps, and community commitment.

A zigzag strategy aims at pushing participation on both sides at the same time, convincing a few customers on both sides at first and using them to convince the others, and then going on from one side to another.

This is the strategy used by YouTube, which at the beginning worked simultaneously on both content producers and viewers, or by Alibaba, which worked on getting Chinese suppliers and foreign buyers on board simultaneously when it first launched.

A two-step approach, instead, aims to get one of the two sides on board first, using it to convince the other to join. This is the strategy leveraged by Open Table. It focused first on signing up restaurants, and then, with enough of them on board, it recruited customers.

Finally, a commitment community strategy is normally useful in those cases in which one of the two sides needs to invest in the platform before joining it, as in the case of game consoles. When the Xbox was launched, Microsoft had to convince developers to invest money to develop games for the console and committed itself to selling the device at a low price to guarantee a critical mass in the user base.

These three strategies are very useful from a theoretical point of view, but practically, how do you solve the chicken-and-egg paradox? Researchers tried to answer this question too, identifying seven tactics (grouped into three clusters) usable to sustain each of the previous strategies (Trabucchi 2020).

Tactics Cluster 1: Stepping Through a One-Sided Platform

This cluster encompasses two possible tactics. The first is called "simulating one side." When implementing this tactic, the platform provider acts to simulate the presence of a customer on the other side to start attracting clients on the first side. BeMyEye is a platform enabling micro mystery client activities on the spot.[2] At the beginning of their story, they published some fake jobs not sponsored by any company but directly financed by the platform to attract gig workers.

This, however, is not the only alternative. Another tactic could be, especially in the case of consumer-to-consumer platforms, to hire— or collaborate with—professionals on the supply side to ensure service delivery from the beginning.

---

[2] The BeMyEye case will be analyzed in a few pages in the paragraph "To grow as much as possible…or to foster quality?"

This is what Ugo did, for example, with another Italian platform when it was called Driver2Home and allowed young people returning from a night at the disco to call someone who could safely drive their car for them.

Today, Ugo is an established platform offering a broader set of services that overcame the chicken-and-egg paradox in this way. This tactic is called the "contract side."

Tactics Cluster 2: One Player for the Other(s)

A second group is called "one player for the others" and can be divided into two different tactics. The first is "involving key players"; the basic idea is to bring onboard a single player who can, however, facilitate the onboarding of both sides. This is what HousingAnywhere did, a platform focused on medium-term rentals, for example, for students going on international mobility: The chicken-and-egg paradox was solved by convincing some universities to come on board, providing both students looking for a room and students offering a room.

The second tactic is "bandwagon effect from the other side"; a great case is that of Qurami, an app that allows queue management by prebooking in crowded offices such as post offices or university secretariats.

The app later became U-First and had a big rollout during the beginning phase of the Covid-19 pandemic in Italy. In this case, by convincing a single customer on the supply side, such as a university secretary's office, you easily bring on board many users on the other side who want to use the secretary's service. Typically, this tactic is useful for bringing the demand side onboard through the supply side.

Tactics Cluster 3: Proper Two-Sided Tactics

The last cluster goes under the name "proper two-sided tactics" and encompasses three different tactics. The first is "direct marketing," often through digital channels, which is very useful when a single advertising message can bring both sides on board, as BlaBlaCar did by buying a lot of advertising space in major French newspapers on the day of a planned strike.

The second is "door to door," the one used by cases like Open Table to bring the first restaurants onboard, literally going door to door to offer the service. Typically, this tactic is more common on the business side.

The third is "leveraging on an existing network" and is, for example, the case of Le Cesarine, a home restaurant platform that overcame the chicken-and-egg paradox by being born from a community of ladies with a passion for cooking who were the first to get on the platform.

These short cases show how overcoming the chicken-and-egg paradox is not easy, but now there are various techniques to try to overcome it, often using different techniques on the two sides, even depending on whether they are consumers or business actors.

So, going back to Alessandro and the early days of Friendz, how did he face the chicken-and-egg paradox?

They selected a *two-step strategy* and implemented it through a *simulating one-side* tactic. They created a large Facebook community of people interested in taking photos and earning credits by taking commissioned photos—from unwitting brands. In other words, the platform created the campaigns as if there was, on the other side, a brand asking for it, but there wasn't. This early phase allowed the company to create a large community with which they could convince brands to get on board as well.

These show how the three strategies can be linked to different tactics that can be used for the single side. They are summarized in Figure 3.1.

Who Pays? How to Create Revenues

When we introduced the concept of "transactional platform " in the previous chapter, we referred to the original label of "two-sided market,"

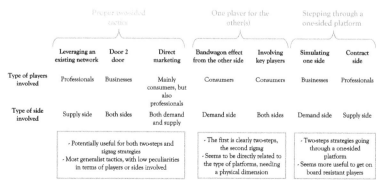

	Proper two-sided tactics			One player for the other(s)		Stepping through a one-sided platform	
	Leveraging an existing network	Door 2 door	Direct marketing	Bandwagon effect from the other side	Involving key players	Simulating one side	Contract side
Type of players involved	Professionals	Businesses	Mainly consumers, but also professionals	Consumers	Consumers	Businesses	Professionals
Type of side involved	Supply side	Both sides	Both demand and supply	Demand side	Both sides	Demand side	Supply side
	· Potentially useful for both two-steps and zigzag strategies · Most generalist tactics, with low peculiarities in terms of players or sides involved			· The first is clearly two-steps, the second zigzag · Seems to be directly related to the type of platforms, needing a physical dimension		· Two-steps strategies going through a one-sided platform · Seems more useful to get on board resistant players	

Figure 3.1 Tactics to approach the chicken-and-egg paradox

which refers to a whole set of studies in the economic world focusing on peculiar cases—like credit cards—and exploring them in depth. Looking back at those studies, especially in the very early days of the 2000s, there was a central topic that gave prominence to the entire field: the pricing strategies of two-sided markets.

If you open a classic marketing book, you can easily find various methods to set the price of a product. Just to mention some, you can start from the product costs (using variable costs and splitting fixed costs on the produced number of products) and add a mark-up, you can use the perceived value that customers have on your product, or you can easily start from the process of competitors (who probably used one of the two previous methods).

Let's try to bring these methods to the platform world.

Let's start with costs. Setting up a platform like Airbnb or Uber has a lot of CAPEX—directly related to the technological platforms,[3] a huge amount of money in the marketing and communication worlds—but almost no OPEX linked to the single transaction.[4] Thus, defining the process starting from costs would mainly mean to split the CAPEX over the number of transactions. Still, with the chicken-and-egg paradox and the role of cross-side network externalities, defining the number of transactions (at least in the early stages) is not feasible.

Similarly, pricing strategies based on the value perceived by customers are not applicable either. The value they perceive depends on the number of players on the other side, and this will become clear only after reaching critical mass. Finally, even looking at competitors' prices is hard for platforms, especially if they open new markets and are not just different versions of already existing platforms.

Common price definition methodologies just don't apply to the platform world. This is again a different job, and, again, it is not an easy one.

---

[3] Capital expenditure or capital expense is the money an organization or corporate entity spends to buy, maintain, or improve its fixed assets, such as buildings, vehicles, equipment, or land.

[4] An operating expense, operating expenditure, operational expense, operational expenditure or OPEX is an ongoing cost for running a product, business, or system.

Basically, transactional platforms are based on a very simple concept: facilitating the meeting between those who are looking for something and those who are offering that something, be they the drivers and passengers of Uber or the travelers and hosts of Airbnb. Thus, to understand something more about who and how much to charge, we can look back to a milestone case that represents the origins of the transactional platform model: eBay.

eBay is probably what comes closest to the oldest case of platform: that of the physical marketplaces we still have in many of our cities. The concept of a marketplace has existed since humans began trading. It is believed that the oldest bazaars were born in Persia, from where they spread throughout the Middle East and Europe. Documentary sources suggest that zoning policies confining trade to parts of cities began around 3,000 BCE, creating the conditions necessary for the emergence of a bazaar.

Middle Eastern bazaars were typically long strips with stalls on either side and a covered roof designed to shade traders and buyers from the sun. In Europe, informal, unregulated markets gradually gave way to a system of formal, licensed markets beginning in the 12th century.

Throughout the medieval period, the increased regulation of market practices, especially weights and measures, gave consumers confidence in the quality of market goods and the fairness of prices. Throughout the world, markets evolved in different ways depending on local environmental conditions, especially weather, tradition, and culture.

The idea, however, is always the same, and it's very close to that of the platforms we mentioned earlier: to bring to the same place—in this case, a physical one, in our examples, a digital one—people looking for and offering something, giving all parties the chance to find someone interested because of the abundance of opportunities in that space.

This means the possibility of having so many sellers, even of very different products, that the buyer going to the market can find virtually everything he is looking for. At the same time, the possibility of having so many potential consumers, go to the market because of the presence of other sellers, means that there is the possibility of turning masses of potential consumers who are at the market into real and paying customers.

Coming back to our modern world, we stopped in California in 1995. It was September 3 when Pierre Omidyar founded AuctionWeb, a place, a market, where people could sell and buy things. It is said that one of the first items sold there was a broken laser pointer for almost $15. He wrote to the buyer, astonished by the fact that it was sold as a broken laser pointer, and he found out that the guy was a collector of broken laser pointers. It soon became the first online auction site to allow peer-to-peer transactions in a wide, digital, and enormous market.

Who pays there? What was the value of eBay back then? Well, at the beginning, the value was very little. It was a personal website, with a few people selling and a few people buying free of charge. At a certain point, Pierre started charging users to sell.

And here we go with the eBay pricing strategy. Buyers are completely free of charge; they do not pay anything to use the service. Sellers do leave a percentage of the price to eBay, usually 12.55 percent (even if today it depends on the seller plan and on the value of the item sold); on top of that, after a set of free of charge listings, they do pay to have a product listed on the platform.

Why do sellers pay, and buyers don't? The answer lies in a specific economic concept: the cross-side elasticity of price (see Parker and Van Alstyne 2005). Simplifying, one side should be subsidized (having the service for free) if the chance to put a price on it would create a significant variation in the willingness (and therefore the numerosity of players) to join the platform, in comparison to what would happen on the other side. Staying on eBay, we can understand from the pricing policies that the impact of adding a fee on the buyer's side would have a much larger (negative) impact than putting it on the seller's side. The chance to subsidize one of the two sides is often used to solve the chicken-and-egg paradox since the subsidized side is easier to convince to join the platform.

This story aims to show you that setting the price on transactional platforms is much more complicated than doing it for a classic product or service. Today, there is a lot more knowledge and experience to build upon, and there are a few typical practices that are used to charge one side in a platform environment. Some of the most commonly used pricing practices are:

- A monthly or entry fee to join the platform, like it happens on the end-user's side in Spotify

- A percentage fee kept by the platform over a happened transaction, as it happens, for example, in Booking.com
- A fixed fee for each transaction, as it happens, for example, with Deliveroo, where the end-users pay a fixed amount of money for each delivery

These three practices can be summed up and even used in various combinations on different sides. For example, Airbnb uses a fixed price strategy per transaction on the traveler's side and keeps a percentage fee on the value of the transaction on the hosts' side. eBay, as we mentioned, used both a fixed and a variable fee strategy on the seller side.

You Can Ask for Help, the Role of Platform Enhancers

Launching a platform is a complex activity. We saw that one of the biggest issues for a transactional platform is the chicken-and-egg paradox, which makes the early stages particularly critical and, very often, a failure to overcome it determines the failure of the whole platform.

What can we do when we're faced with situations that are too complex to handle on our own? Very often, we overcome these difficulties by collaborating. Even in the world of platforms, it often happens to see a joint effort in the launch of a new reality.

To tell you about this aspect, we decided to use an Italian case, which was wanted by the government and happened similarly in other countries also. This is SPID, the Italian platform for digital identity management.

SPID means "Sistema pubblico per l'identità digitale," which in English sounds like "Public system for the digital identity." It is a joint project by AgID and DTT, two government agencies, which act as platform providers with mostly control and regulatory roles (Figure 3.2).

SPID provides Italian citizens with a unique and secure digital identity, allowing them to trustfully authenticate and access the online services offered by public and private entities, which can be defined as service providers. It is thus a platform that matches citizens (first side), who need a unique set of credentials to seamlessly access different online services, with the providers of these services (second side), who strive to enlarge

Citizens   Service providers

Figure 3.2 The case of SPID

their customer base and manage it with a highly secure and frictionless authentication method.

We are talking about a national reality, wanted by the government, which can significantly help in the launch of a platform and in overcoming the chicken-and-egg paradox. Nevertheless, as often happens in the world of platforms, a service of this type only makes sense and has value if it is widespread. This was the practical difficulty of launching a platform like SPID.

The identity, before becoming digital, must be verified by a person. This is already challenging but not enough. The service is wanted by the government and must be accessible to everybody. Thus, to verify the identity, physical spaces spread across the territory were also needed, to overcome the digital divide and make the service available to that part of the population with low digital skills.

AgID and DTT could have developed a large, widespread network of physical registration points across the country, investing a considerable amount of public money, but instead, they asked other players for help.

A series of private players, having already a wide and transversal access to the public, were involved in the project with the role of identity providers. We are talking about companies like Poste Italiane, the Italian mailing system, TIM, of the largest telecommunication service provider and many others.

These companies have the role of facilitating one step of the value creation of the platform, in this case, the control of the real identity to assign the unique digital one. In getting on board the SPID project, however, it is important to underline that they do not act as members of the second side. When they offer the ability to access their services through SPID, they manage a portion of the activities that enable future transactions between end-users and all service providers. In other words, with their role as identity providers, they are not generating new cross-side or cross-network externalities, but they are taking care of a (critical) operational side of the platform provider service. In other words, the SPID platform outsourced a critical activity to external partners who had assets (their physical presence on the territory) to provide effective and rapid operations. It is quite easy to understand why the SPID platform was interested in this partnership (saving money and time to set up the system), but what did the partners gain? The SPID platform was able to create a win-win-win-win mechanism around the platform ecosystem.

The SPID platform had a win situation because it didn't invest in the identification system and had it managed by identity providers without paying them (otherwise, the investment savings would have been waived).

The citizens had a win situation because they were offered a physical identification service for free.

The identity providers had a win situation because, despite the identities being totally free for all Italian citizens and besides public administrations not paying for the authentication to their online services on the SPID platform, they could sell citizens further services to complement the SPID (cross-selling), such as digital signatures, and can be paid by private service providers in the SPID platform for authentication in their services.

Finally, private service providers on the SPID platform have a win situation because, besides paying for the authentication of their services on the SPID platform, they can dismiss their proprietary systems and avoid further investments in their improvement.

This case allows us to show a new role that should be considered when we design the launch of a new platform; actors such as identity providers take the name of platform enhancers (Trabucchi et al. 2018).

A platform enhancer is an organization that cooperates with the platform provider to launch and run a new platform, providing crucial support to the management of the chicken-and-egg paradox. They do not generate network externalities regarding any of the sides (the value perceived by none of the sides, in this case citizens and service providers, is linked to the number of identity providers), but they perform part of the work of the platform relying on their assets and resources (Figure 3.3). Their relationship with the platform provider is based on a defined

Citizens   Service providers

Figure 3.3 The case of SPID with the platform enhancers

value proposition of a collaborative nature, even if they do not own the platform.

The chance of involving platform enhancers has the benefit of collaborating with other companies, potentially exploiting their network and their market positioning, in one of the most delicate phases of the life cycle of a platform: its launch. Obviously, this makes the management of an already complex and varied system even more complex by including new stakeholders into the ecosystem.

To Grow as Much as Possible or to Foster Quality?

Launching a platform is not a simple job; we have seen this with the chicken-and-egg paradox and all the strategies and tactics to overcome it, as well as in the difficulties in setting the price.

Unfortunately, once the platform is launched, we are again not in front of a simple entity to manage. Platforms are based on a balance between the sides, between the work that the platform does and the work that customers do in their various roles. The platform provider's task is then to manage the platform in its maturity phase, balancing the sides or adding new ones to complement the existing offer and leverage new opportunities.

The first aspect we want to address in relation to this issue is the customers that get on the platform, whether they are on the demand or supply side, asking for or offering something in the platform world.

We know that we need many of them to activate network externalities and reach a sufficient critical mass to start growing—but is quantity the only driver?

Let's go on with our journey; we are back in Italy in 2011. This is the story of BeMyEye, a platform that has gained huge relevance all over

Europe, even though its brand is not that popular with consumers—and we will understand why.

BeMyEye was founded by Gianluca Petrelli. As it often happens, he started with a simple observation of a daily situation. In those months, Gianluca made a commercial agreement with some American supermarkets for the promotion of an Italian olive oil brand.

He wondered if the money spent to access a specific position on the market shelf or on posters was well spent. He knew that, being on another continent, it was virtually impossible to check if the agreements were being respected, if the bottles were shown in the right stand, and if the posters were shown in the stores. Everything changed when he realized that many people were in that same moment in those supermarkets and could easily send him a picture with their smartphone to show if and how the agreements had been respected.

From this simple consideration, he created BeMyEye, the platform that allows companies to give small tasks, related to the retail world, that can be solved with a photo or a similar action by anyone who wants to receive a small amount of money back. The demand side is companies, and the supply side is eyes—those who want to accomplish at least one of these tasks. BeMyEye is now a leader in its sector in Europe. They created an established network of customers on the demand side.

Here we go with the key point of this story. What would happen if tomorrow BeMyEye was downloaded by millions of users, maybe concentrated in a specific geographical area, let's say, for example, Milan? In a very short amount of time, all these "eye providers" would destroy the value of the platform. This is highly counterintuitive (we always talked about the cross-network externalities and the scalability of the system), but it is true. In fact, if the customer base grows too quickly and too soon in a confined geographical area, hardly could the number of tasks to be performed grow as fast, and probably, in some cases, it would never grow enough even having more time. A system with eyes but no tasks would rapidly collapse. Moreover, this might create asymmetries and malfunctioning also on the suppliers' side. The same company might see the mission launched in Milan immediately fulfilled, while a similar mission launched in another city with fewer "eyes" might take much longer time to complete or even remain incomplete.

This example allows us to highlight two crucial points.

Point 1: Platforms are not all the same. A service like BeMyEye has specific characteristics, like other cases such as BlaBlaCar, but is completely different from others, like eBay, for example. First, there is a physical, geographical dimension to the platform, even though it is a digital service. A company might require hundreds of missions of the same type, scattered across the country, so the presence of eyes in large cities but also in smaller towns becomes crucial. Second, there is a temporal nature to the service. The match must necessarily take place in a reasonable amount of time. This is not true for all platforms, but it allows us to see how variables, such as the physical size of the service or being based on durable goods (like Airbnb rooms) or one-shot services (like BlaBlaCar or BeMyEye), have significant implications on the platform management.

Point 2: Quantity is not the holy grail of platforms, and the balance between the two sides requires careful management. Each platform must have a certain type of balance between the two sides, and the case of BeMyEye tells us how it is also necessary to choose, at least partially, who goes on one of the two sides. In other words, in addition to the quantity of customers on one side, it is also important to consider their quality. Some actors are more valuable to the platform than others because they possess certain characteristics, which in the case of BeMyEye are mainly their geographical location.

Quality of the customers is not just another variable to be taken into consideration; in some stages of the mature life of a platform, it can even become more important than quantity, and it is up to the platform provider to understand when the two variables exchange their roles and implement concrete actions to manage the balance. In the case of BeMyEye, the company decided to never do generalist marketing campaigns to directly increase the number of eyes without control. They, instead, activated Facebook ads in a spot way, precisely in the areas where new eyes were needed.

Similar dynamics happen in many platforms. An interesting case is that of Friendz. You read about the Friendz case earlier in this chapter; well, they had a similar path regarding quality. Friendz asks users to take photos of products and post them on social networks to do micro-influencing for brands that pay the platform for this service. In this case, the quality of the photo is a crucial variable. On the one hand, there is a filter managed by the staff that controls the photos. Still, on the other hand, they work to increase the quality of their providers. They developed a process, based on nonbranded campaigns, that helps users, through a gamified mechanism, to constantly improve their abilities and the quality of their photos.

In conclusion, there is not a single answer to the dilemma of quantity versus quality, but the two strategies are often followed over time (Trabucchi et al. 2021a).

A focus on quantity, often combined with a mechanism—such as feedback or filters at the entrance—aimed at creating a minimum quality or that keeps the system healthy by eliminating negative behaviors from the various sides, is useful in the early stages of the life of a platform, to reach critical mass and begin to grow by overcoming the chicken-and-egg paradox. At the same time, a focus on quality can be useful in the maturity phase, even taking on different forms:

- Quality as a good mix: As in the case of Deliveroo where sometimes the value added by a new restaurant can even have a negative effect on the value perceived by customers. For example, adding a pizzeria when there are 10 others in the same area might not increase the perceived value to customers but only make it more difficult for them to select the one they want. Maybe adding a sushi restaurant instead, if they are not in the area, might be a much more valuable choice to increase the value perceived by the final customer.
- Quality as the right one: As in the case of BeMyEye, looking for the perfect customers to keep the match between the two sides balanced, in that case based on geographical location.
- Quality as a process: As in the case of Friendz with gamification, going to create an experience on the platform that allows those who go there to reach a higher level of quality in the activity they do.

Evolving the Platform Through New Transactions

So far, we have focused on transactional platforms with two sides and the difficulties they have, especially in the early days. Still, this is an innovation book. What does it mean for two-sided transactional platforms to foster innovation? What must platform thinkers consider once they reach a stable maturity phase with the two sides onboard and a lot of transactions happening and sustaining the cross-side network externalities?

If we look at large established platforms, we can easily see how they are particularly difficult to read through the pure platform models we introduced (for more tactics over the life cycle, see Trischler et al. 2021). Companies like Facebook or Amazon orchestrate a complex network of relationships among many different sides.

Facebook was born with the aim of putting in contact different people who are looking for each other. Today, however, the platform created by Zuckerberg also enables many other transactions, having on board companies, developers, advertisers, and other players. Amazon, in a completely similar way, in addition to buyers and sellers in its marketplace, offers services to customers who buy its computing capacity, sells advertising spaces on its marketplace, and produces and distributes movies and TV series.

How can a platform go from being a transactional, two-sided platform that connects two groups of customers, such as Amazon's sellers and buyers, to being a large, multisided platform with multiple customer groups or multiple services offered to those sides? We will now introduce some strategies to let transactional, two-sided platforms evolve through the introduction of new transaction lines.

Service Enlargement and Platform Gemini

A first, simple way to allow a transactional, two-sided platform to have new transactions is by enabling the sides already on the platform to interact in a new way. We call this strategy simple "service enlargement," as it represents an evolution of what a platform is offering to the customers that are already on board.

A great example can come from one of the companies that we have already met in this chapter: eBay. As we previously mentioned, the marketplace was founded in 1995 as AuctionWeb, basing its value proposition on the idea that anyone could sell there an object not at a fixed price but to the best bidder. In September 1997, it was rebranded as eBay and began to grow significantly over the years, becoming the greatest success story of the dotcom bubble. In July 1999, it started the global expansion, launching its service in Germany, Australia, and the United Kingdom, while in 2000 it started applying the service enlargement.

In November 2000, the feature Buy it Now, a new fixed-price feature that allows users to buy an item instantly at a set price, was introduced. The platform is the same, with the same old buyers and sellers, but a new kind of service that can match the two through a transaction.

Similar to what we just introduced with the service enlargement, we may follow a similar expansion logic at the platform level.

Consider, for example, Amazon Prime Video, which is a subscription service offered by Amazon as a standalone service, despite what is happening on the Amazon marketplace.

The service primarily distributes movies and TV shows produced by Amazon Studios or licensed to Amazon as Amazon Originals. Still, it also hosts content from other providers, content add-ons, live sporting events, and video rental and purchasing services. Prime Video additionally offers a content add-on service in the form of channels, called Amazon Channels, or Prime Video Channels, that allow users to subscribe to additional video subscription services from other content providers within Prime Video. This is making Prime Video a transactional two-sided platform, having viewers on the first side and content providers on the second. Nevertheless, in terms of platform evolution, it is interesting to see how they got there.

It was launched on September 7, 2006, in the United States, as Amazon Unbox, then became Amazon Instant Video on Demand, and then, after acquiring the U.K.-based streaming and DVD-by-mail service Love-Film in 2011, it became Prime Video as part of the Prime subscription in various countries. The Prime subscription is an Amazon service that offers faster delivery for a selected set of products. On April 18, 2016, Amazon split Prime Video from Amazon Prime in the United States for $8.99 per month and then in many other countries. This evolution makes Prime Video a perfect case of "platform gemini." The two sides—the viewers and the content providers—are mainly already present on the Amazon platform, acting as demand side (buying products) and supply side (e.g., selling DVDs of their movies) in the Amazon Marketplace, but the company decided to create for them a new platform for a different set of transactions.

Supply-Side Addition and Demand-Side Addition

A common strategy related to the evolution of transactional two-sided platforms is related to the introduction of new supply sides. This approach is therefore called supply-side addition (Trabucchi and Buganza 2020) (Figure 3.4). To introduce it, we can start with the observation of an emblematic case in the world of platforms: Airbnb.

The platform was founded in 2008 with the goal of connecting people looking for a place to stay and people who wanted to offer a bed. In late 2016, the platform began to expand, adding a third group of customers: experience providers, people who offer services through which travelers, the first-side customers, can live different experiences in the cities where they are, such as bike rides or cooking classes. Conceptually, this move is as if the platform provider decides to create a new two-sided platform, connecting travelers with experience providers. Still, they did not begin from scratch; there was not a new chicken-and-egg paradox. They started with a semiprocessed platform that already has the first side on board.

This is an example of supply-side addition because they added a new supply side to the one already presented in the initial structure, but, from a value perspective, the platform enables a new transaction between experience providers and travelers. In this way, the platform provider can leverage the existing community to enable new externalities right away, offering high externalities immediately to the new third side (experience providers). This strategy can then be implemented repeatedly, resulting in even particularly complex systems with many sides. Airbnb is an excellent example of adding a third side with a transactional logic, but we can find many others, such as Uber with restaurants and Uber Eats (we will talk about it later, in Chapter 6).

First transactional side (end-users)

Platform provider

Third transactional side

Second transactional side

Figure 3.4 Supply-side addition

We think it's useful to mention another company that has made supply-side addition a successful and repeated strategy. We are talking about Grab. Grab Holdings is a multinational company headquartered in Singapore.

The idea of creating a taxi-booking mobile app for Southeast Asia, like those being pioneered in the United States, first came from Anthony Tan while he was at Harvard Business School.

Motivated to make taxi rides safer in Malaysia, Tan launched the "My Teksi" app in Malaysia in 2012 together with Tan Hooi Ling, another Harvard graduate. My Teksi started with an initial grant of U.S. $25,000 from Harvard Business School and Anthony Tan's personal capital.

The name changed to GrabTaxi, and the company expanded to the Philippines in August 2013, and to Singapore and Thailand in October of the same year. In May 2014, to overcome the lack of public transportation during peak hours, the company launched GrabCar as an alternative form of transportation that uses personal cars instead of taxis. This is the first example of a supply-side addition that will lead to many more. In November 2014, GrabTaxi launched its first GrabBike service in Ho Chi Minh City as a trial service. Today, Grab has many sides, offering various types of services, from transportation—with taxis or private cars—to food or other product delivery, tickets for shows, hotels, and other subscription services.

Grab became a sort of service hub in Asia by merging many of the platforms we used as examples in this course—always leveraging supply-side additions.

The cases of Airbnb Experiences and the various evolutions of Grab clearly deal with the supply side of the original transactional two-sided platform. Nevertheless, the side addition is not necessarily an evolution strategy related to the supply side. Let's consider, for example, Deliveroo, the British food delivery company founded by Will Shu and Greg Orlowski in 2013 in London. Their basic and initial service is easily mapped into a transactional, two-sided platform: They enable transactions between end-users who wish to enjoy a restaurant-like meal from home and restaurants. Their model proved to be successful, becoming one of the European unicorns. Still, in 2016, they introduced "Deliveroo for Business," the B2B version of the original service, welcoming companies on board as demand sides. The service offered is slightly different, since companies may pick among three main alternatives: events (which offer catering), hotels (which offer accommodations and room service to their guests), and fruit baskets (which offer the chance to receive baskets with fruits and snacks for meetings or other collective gatherings). The mechanism is the same as that of the previous examples but works on the demand side: it is a demand-side addition.

Platform Thinking World: The MOOC "Designing a Platform"

This chapter also lives as an entire course we developed, produced by METID Politecnico di Milano, and freely available on Coursera; check it out: "Platform Thinking: Designing a Platform" (Figure 3.5).

Figure 3.5 QR code for the platform thinking MOOC "Designing a Platform"

Source: bit.ly/PT_MOOC_2.

CHAPTER 4

The Role of Data in Platform Thinking

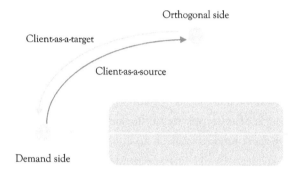

We Live in the Era of the Freeconomics

Year 2000. The life of any teenager in the world was made of choices. Many choices were driven by economic availability and the willingness to maximize the value captured. To buy a CD could take up to €20 or even €25. The price was for a full package of 12 songs on average, many of which were not as good as the lead single. To buy a DVD, the price was comparable; a night to the movies was about €10, a magazine €6 to €7, and a newspaper €1.

Today, we still enjoy the same things but, they look like free. Using Spotify, you can access millions of songs for free or something like 9€ per month if you wish a premium service. Netflix, for less than €10, gives you thousands of titles available whenever you want. Any social media can lead you to continuous up-to-date news for free.

We are getting used to not paying for what we get or anyhow to pay very little money for something that we used to pay way more. We are living in the economy of free services, and there is a word to describe it: freeconomics.

The term "freeconomics" was invented to describe the point at which the spread of nuclear energy would have made electricity "too cheap to meter."

We have yet to reach that point in the energy industry, but a similar scenario is not far from reality in digital industries.

The cost of processing power, storage, bandwidth, and other technologies connected to the digital revolution decreases following the so-called Moore's law. As a result, the computing power is rapidly becoming "too cheap to meter," making it possible for some businesses to offer digital services for free and harvest value in other ways.

Facebook, for instance, has billions of monthly active users, none of whom pays anything to enjoy its services. Facebook makes money by allowing third-party companies to access users' newsfeeds, through advertising and business pages.

Google and all its services, from the search engine to Street View, from Translator to Google Scholar, operate in the same way—advertisers pay the cost of making those services available to users for free.

These companies leverage an old business model, dating from the beginnings of the modern newspaper industry: advertising.

As we mentioned in Chapter 2, the advertising-based model is a specific type of two-sided platform approach in which free (or almost free) services are delivered to large numbers of consumers, who then become targets for the advertisers who pay to access their eyeballs. In terms of business models, this approach is classified as an orthogonal two-sided platform with a "client-as-target" strategy (Figure 4.1).

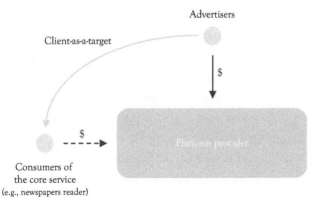

Figure 4.1 Orthogonal platforms (client-as-a-target)

This is still one of the most popular value-capturing mechanisms in the world of digital services and the main revenue generation mechanism for most of the digital giants.

As this approach proliferated across the Internet and app field, customers started expecting all digital services to be free—even those they might pay for in the physical world. To escape this equation "digital service equals free services," new models for value capturing emerged, such as:

- Freemium models, which mix free basic services with paid premium ones; as in the case of Spotify where you can have access to the service, with some limitations, for free or pay a monthly fee to get the full experience.
- In-app purchase models, which give the basic app away but offer users opportunities to enrich their experience with it through paid add-ons; this is the typical case of many games in the app world, such as Pokémon Go, that is totally free, but to have more digital objects in the game and to have the chance to play longer without going around, or simply to be more successful in the game, you can buy digital products in the virtual world.
- Cross-selling models, in which the free app goes along with a physical product to be sold on the market, such as Fitbit's companion mobile app to its physical fitness tracker: you pay the tracker once, while the service related to the app can be free potentially forever.

These models offer new ways to capture value from innovations in a world dominated by "free," but none of them fits comfortably into an environment in which customers are increasingly used not to pay for what they get. Advertising is a valuable alternative for sure, but advertising companies must then sell their services to companies with revenues, otherwise the game doesn't work. We cannot expect advertisers to pay for everything we use in a free world. Thus, the question of whether there is a sustainable way to offer digital services for free, besides advertising, becomes crucial.

There is a common point shared by all the digital services mentioned: the fact of being apps on a smartphone lets them gather a huge amount and variety of data. Data originated as a by-product of the main service are digital waste of the main service—but that proved to be very valuable from a business model perspective.

Several companies began to explore the value of these data; we mentioned in Chapter 2 the case of Twitter that in 2009 started selling the access to its database of tweets to third parties, many of whom generated insights from it through sentiment analysis to understand the general mood or reaction to events or politicians from the tweet stream. That was just the beginning of the rise of orthogonal two-sided platforms, with a client-as-a-source strategy (Figure 4.2).

The Twitter Political Index, presented during the 2012 U.S. presidential election, is just one example of the potential for Twitter's data stream to support powerful insights. In this way, the company created a new and powerful revenue stream. Google, Facebook, and many others have experimented with similar approaches, capturing economic value from the data generated by users.

Many questions remain: how is it possible that digital companies capture such a huge value through data? What are these data? Where are they coming from?

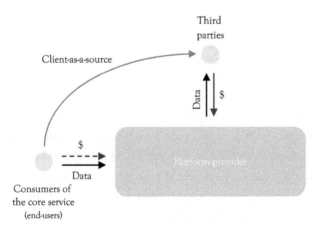

Figure 4.2 Orthogonal platforms (client-as-a-source)

The Rise of Data-Driven Personalized Services—Driven by the iPhone

January 9, 2007. In this day, we can position the beginning of a great revolution, which in a few years led to a world very different from the one we knew. That day, during the MacWorld conference, Steve Jobs presented the iPhone, Apple's first smartphone. We can consider that day as day 0 of a revolution that is still going on.

The iPhones, but more in general all smartphones and the various smart devices that followed in subsequent years, are the enablers of this great data-driven revolution.

Smartphones transformed phones from a tool for making phone calls to a concentration of sensors such as a camera, GPS, accelerometer, microphone, and touch screen, which enabled the generation of different types of data in a single tool (Figure 4.3).

Steve Jobs, sensing the potential of his new product, launched shortly after the App Store.[1] Doing so, he allowed anyone who wanted to develop

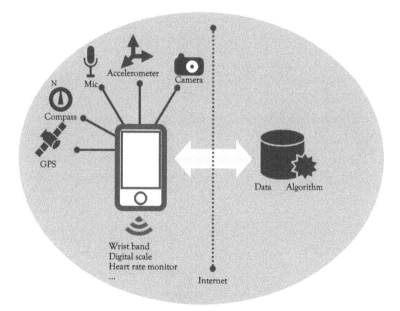

Figure 4.3 The smartphone as the gate for data generation

---

[1] Steve Jobs Introduces the App store—iPhone SDK Keynote. https://youtu.be/xo9cKe_Fch8.

new services for the iPhone users. In a few years, the smartphone become a
real gateway between the real world, which it studies and analyzes through its
sensors, and the virtual world, in which it reports the results of these analyses.

Some examples? We mentioned Waze in Chapter 1, the app that played
a fundamental role in the spread of smartphone navigators challenging the
leadership of TomTom and Garmin. Waze transformed the concept of navigators from a tool you use only when you must reach a place you don't
know, to that tool that helps you reach any place—even those you know
where they are—in the fastest way and avoiding traffic. This change was
possible because of data collected through the sensors on the smartphones.
The accelerometer and GPS actively monitor the speed of the car and,
together with the user's own signals and the data coming from other users
on the same road, allow Waze to generate real-time and personalized suggestions to reach any given location. Another example comes from fitness
tracking services, such as Runkeeper or Runtastic. These apps track users
as they run; analyze their pace, speed, and breaks; and develop customized
training plans that meet the individual's needs and objectives.

All of this, which has become increasingly common in various digital
services, is made possible by combining three different sources of data
(Figure 4.4):

1. End-user inputs: like when we tell Waze where we want to go, or
   tell a fitness tracker how many miles we want to run, our weight, or
   our height
2. The data coming from the smartphone and its sensors: for example,
   the speed in the two previous examples or our current geographical
   position

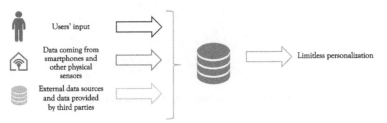

Figure 4.4 The data inputs for limitless personalization

3. The data coming from external sources or third parties that can enrich the previous information, for example, the temperature or the percentage of humidity while we are running—recoverable thanks to the position given by the GPS and the time

All these data feed databases that, thanks to algorithms based mainly on artificial intelligence, can give life to a sort of limitless personalization; in other words they allow millions of users to have highly personalized services for free (see Buganza et al. 2020). All we must do to trigger this magic is to give away a small amount of our data to the service provider.

We can identify two main variables in these services, which allow us to have a classification.

- The degree of interaction and participation, in other words, how active the user must be to have a personalized service
- The degree of user contact, when the service observes—even in the background—the direct behavior of the user

If both variables are low, we have "background monitoring services," such as Nest, the smart thermostat that leveraging our very simple and limited inputs (the desired temperature) creates a personalized profile of the heating of our home by observing our behavior (when we are home, at what time we go to sleep, etc.)—and claims to reduce our heating expenses by nearly 20 percent.

A second group is that of "threshold-call services," such as Credit Karma, which observes the user's financial behavior and only requires the customer intervention in specific situations.

Both variables are high in the case of "digital coaches," where algorithms observe in real time the user's behavior to adapt the user experience at that moment, as in the case of Duolingo that personalizes the experience of learning a language on the go.

The last particularly interesting case is that of "virtual real seamless services," with a low degree of user involvement but a high degree of background observation, as in the case of Waze. These services seem to make the real magic. They offer a quasi-limitless personalization requiring low or even no active work by the customer enabling a continuous cross-reference between real world and virtual reality through data.

This classification shows us how data have already enabled so many different services, involving the user in a direct way but offering highly personalized experiences (Figure 4.5).

As we said at the beginning, these services are often free or almost free: how is this possible? What is the value-capturing mechanism that these companies put in place? As you might imagine, the answer lies in between the typology of platforms, orthogonal two-sided platforms with a client-as-a-source logic. In the next sections, we will explore these strategies.

Before moving on, a very important notice: we will describe value-capturing mechanisms based on the usage of data. Data usage is probably the most debated topic on digital platforms and one of the aspects used against platforms. By the end of the chapter, we will also discuss these controversies—even if they are not the central topic of the book—to give you the widest view possible on platforms.

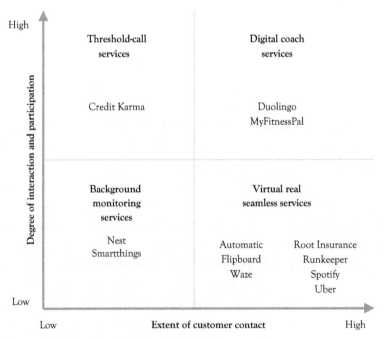

Figure 4.5 The classification of data-driven service

Still, a disclaimer before moving on is necessary. We will be talking about models that are always coherent with the governmental regulations, such as the GDPR in Europe, and ensure the privacy of the end-users. The three models described in the next three sections were first studied in a paper published in 2017 (Trabucchi et al. 2017), based on the analyses of the privacy policies of a set of digital apps, again to highlight the compliance of these models with the current regulation. Obviously, this disregards any reasoning on ethics and consumer awareness that we will discuss later in the chapter.

In the remaining of the chapter, we will dig into the usage of various ways to exploit data to capture value through orthogonal platforms mechanisms, starting from the ones based purely on a client-as-a-source strategy and the ones that rely also on the client-as-a-target one.

Pure Client-as-a-Source Strategy

Platform-Oriented e-Ethnography and Side-Oriented e-Ethnography

The iPhone can be considered the cornerstone of the models we're talking about—the first major enabler of thousands of digital services that have figured out how to leverage data from its sensors to capture, and not just create, value.

It's interesting to see how, in this story, Apple has an even more primordial role, with one of its first, and most iconic, partnerships back in the days of the iPod: Nike+.

Before becoming one of the most famous mobile apps on the planet, Nike+ (now NRC) was a sensor chip to be inserted in the shoes and connected to the iPod. It was the antecedent to all the sport mobile apps that leverage data coming from the smartphone sensors.

The sensor and iPod kit were revealed on May 20, 2006. The kit stored information such as the elapsed time of the workout, the distance traveled, pace, and calories burned by the individual. Nike+ was a collaboration between Nike and Apple; the platform consisted of an iPod, a wireless chip, Nike shoes that accepted the wireless chip, an iTunes membership, and a Nike+ online community.

As a logical development, on September 7, 2010, Nike released the Nike+ Running App on the App Store, which used a tracking engine powered by

MotionX that did not require the separate shoe sensor or pedometer. This application worked using the accelerometer and GPS of the iPhone and the accelerometer of the iPod Touch, which does not have a GPS chip.

During our research into the business models of free apps, such as Nike+, we studied privacy policies as a means of understanding whether and how these companies might use the data collected by the apps. And in the case of Nike+, we found a pleasant surprise. Unlike many other cases, in this case, there was explicit mention that the data collected would not be used for advertising purposes or given to third parties but could be used within the company, and not just in the digital subsidiary Nike Digital.

As Stefan Olander, Nike's vice president of Digital Sport, told an interviewer,

> The opportunity that is presenting itself right now is completely different. The relationships we have [with the customer], and this is something we learned from Nike+ already, are so much more impactful when someone comes back to the brand two or three times a week to sync a run, versus what it used to be which was convince someone that we had something amazing—which we do—then you buy it and you have a great experience with the product but we don't know anything about that experience.[2]

In other words, user data are a precious source of valuable insights into users' habits, needs, and interactions with the company's products; user data streams allow for large-scale observation of thousands or even millions of user interactions with a product. Further, these observations are noninvasive since they are embedded in the user's experience. Where the app supports a physical product, the benefits can extend far beyond the app itself. Nike uses its Nike+ Running customers to understand how people use its core product: shoes. App users provide a huge amount of information about their workout habits that allows the company to profile its customers and understand critical attributes. For instance, the company may know things like the fact that men in their late 30s run an average of 37.8 km/week, with an average single run distance of 6.2 km at an average pace of 6.56 per

---

[2] Wired Business Conference: Testing Your Limits. https://youtu.be/5p9P SqVjXBQ.

mile. Most people run mainly on Sundays and the most frequently selected "power song" is "Eye of the Tiger." All these possible insights can be gleaned from data gathered through the app. The relevance these data can have for an established company can explain the absence of direct revenue sources for some of the apps we studied—these apps may exist primarily to provide support for the core business, rather than to generate direct revenue, by providing data from which the company can glean valuable insights about how its customers interact with the physical product.

In other terms, the platform consists of Nike+ Running, the mobile app released and distributed by the digital division of Nike, and has two customers: the end-users, the runners, and the overall company itself that uses the data. In this case, the strategy is purely client-as-a-source and it is basically within the firm, involving different functions or part of the organization, but still generating cross-side network externalities, since the value of these data is directly related to the number of data points.

This strategy takes the name of platform-oriented e-ethnography (Figure 4.6), inspired by the world of ethnography, the methodology born in the anthropological field, observing the various populations to understand their behaviors. In business, we talk about applied ethnography, and it's a methodology commonly used in market-push innovation, observing the user to understand how she uses a product to propose innovations that tend to be incremental and satisfy emerging needs.

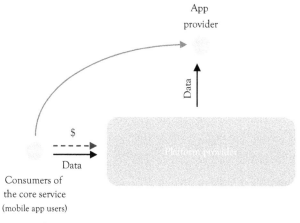

Figure 4.6 e-ethnography

This is exactly what happens in this type of platform, observing—albeit in the background, hence the name e-ethnography—the user and having the possibility to innovate the core products based on the insights collected.

This mechanism, the information collected on the usage of a product such as in this case shoes, allows capturing value without direct monetization, justifying the free service.

It's not easy to find examples of companies using apps in this way, as there's often no clear evidence of it from the outside, but it's important to consider it among the strategies we can use to capture value from the data in a platform.

Another example? It seems that Netflix uses data on its users' habits and the programs they watch, when they pause, how long it takes them to finish a series, and what basket of movies and TV series a person sees, not only to decide whether to renew a series, but also to understand what kind of products users are looking for, turning them into valuable inputs for generating new contents. The declaration on the decision to bid on the American version of House of Cards became popular, after seeing the pilot episode directed by David Fincher and played by Kevin Spacey. In Netflix, they had the chance to analyze the results of the English version of House of Cards and to match those data with the performances of the previous movies by David Fincher and of the previous movies starring Kevin Spacey:

> We have a high degree of confidence in [House of Cards] based on the director, the producer, and the stars…. We don't have to spend millions to get people to tune into this. Through our algorithms, we can determine who might be interested in Kevin Spacey or political drama and say to them "You might want to watch this." (Steve Swasey, VP of Corporate Communications, in an interview with Gigaom)[3]

This is an early example of how the data gathered through the main service influenced the production function in Netflix to pick or not to

---

[3] R. Lawlr. 2011. *How Netflix Will Use Big Data to Push House of Cards.* https://gigaom.com/2011/03/18/netflix-big-data/.

pick a series. Similar reasonings followed for which original content to create, what to renew for more seasons, and so on.

Nike+ and Netflix are great cases of platform-oriented e-ethnography since they rely on the power of data to offer a service to another area of the organization they are offered by. Still, the power of data may go far beyond that and may be perused also for other players in the platform ecosystem. That is the case of Spotify. Spotify is a transactional two-sided platform which connects listeners to artists. Leveraging the data collected during the delivery of the service, they created in 2013 a specific add-on service called Spotify for Artist, to offer a set of insights to the artists about how listeners enjoy their songs, for how long, after how long they change songs, and so on. In other words, they have opened data to artists, helping them to understand the value embedded in what Spotify knows about the streams they get. They developed an ad hoc value proposition for the service, which is "Spotify for Artists helps you to develop the fanbase you need to reach your goals." This approach to data usage—different from others—does not generate new revenues or even reduce costs (ad in the case of platform-oriented e-ethnography) but mainly generates engagement and value of one of the sides, feeding their willingness to stay on the platform, and therefore the cross-side network externalities with the other side. We label this as side-oriented e-ethnography, a strategy that aims to generate a data-driven value-added service for one of the sides, exploiting the value of data that are already there, while increasing the value perceived by the customers on one of the sides.

Data Trading

Have you ever heard the case of Strava? Strava is a San Francisco-based company founded in 2009 by Mark Gainey and Michael Horvath, delivering a sports app service which incorporates social networking features. It is mostly used for cycling and leverages GPS data from tracking devices, most commonly smartphones. Strava adopts a freemium model with some features only available in the paid subscription plan.

Now imagine the following situation. You and a colleague are at the Strava headquarters in the early 2010s. Strava is a fast-growing startup and you're still incredulous about the success and spread of the app you've been working on.

On a normal afternoon at the office, you thought about mapping the data you've collected over the past few months onto a map of San Francisco. In short, you thought of a way to visualize what each user sees at the end of a workout—the route they took on the map—in a single map that would consider all users in San Francisco and the time they took that route. In jargon, it's called a heat map, and it allows you to see which areas and times are most densely populated by cyclists in the city.

This computer exercise generates a moment of pure fun with your colleague: moving a cursor, you can see how the city's users are concentrated mainly in certain areas and, for example, how the trends are different between weekdays—in which we can imagine many people use the bike to go to work and then go downtown—and weekends, in which we see much longer average routes and a strong concentration in city parks.

Imagine being in front of this screen with your colleague and being happy with the result, knowing how people move around the city using the bike and feel that excitement you normally feel when you finish programming an application and see the result working.

Once the tech euphoria has passed, imagine your colleague turning to you and saying, "Well, that's nice, but what do we do with it now? Who cares where people in San Francisco ride their bikes?"

We don't know if that was the conversation, but that's the right question for building a platform that can capture the value of a digital application's data. Who cares about the data we have? To whom are they valuable?

A brain-storming session probably led to the right answer: the transportation departments of the various municipalities.

Strava Metro is a new service to supply customers (mostly municipalities) packages of data on how people move around the city, allowing them to make data-driven decisions about, for example, where to build new bike lanes or where to make investment. The magazine *Wired* in 2013 reported one of the first deals struck is with the Oregon Department of Transportation, which bought an annual data package from Strava for $20,000, a far cry from the typical $5 monthly fee for a freemium subscription.[4] Since then, Strava Metro became another line of business for

---

[4] A. Davies. 2014. *Strava's Cycling App Is Helping Cities Build Better Bike Lanes.* www.wired.com/2014/06/strava-sells-cycling-data/.

Strava, transforming a linear value chain company into a pure two-sided orthogonal platform.

Strava is the platforms provider; the first side is represented by the end-users, the cyclists, who are, at the same time, the customers and the company data factory. The second side is represented by all the third parties that see value in these (aggregated) data, such as the various departments of transportation. As in the previous cases, this is a case of a client-as-a-source strategy, where the first side enjoys the service for free (or freemium) but is also the main source of the value (data factory) that will then be offered to the orthogonal side, again generating unidirectional cross-side network externalities. After a couple of years, Strava decided to open Strava Metro for free as a corporate social responsibility project.

This strategy is called "data trading" (Figure 4.7)—data can be sold, or even simply exchanged with other data, as Waze did back in the years with the municipality of Rome, exchanging data on the traffic in the city.[5]

This is the most complex strategy for capturing value through data collected with a digital application because it requires the platform's ability to understand who might be interested in those data and how to make them useful and actionable. Here we can more easily find various

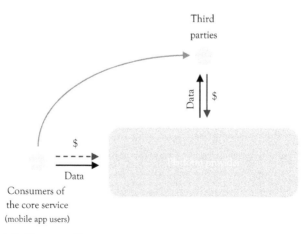

Figure 4.7 Data trading

[5] D. Parlangeli. 2016. *A Roma il Comune parla con Waze per gestire il traffic.* www.wired.it/mobile/app/2016/05/12/roma-waze/.

examples, as we mentioned, Twitter sells tweet streams for search purposes, and Uber and Skyscanner do something similar. Uber created a service, so far for free, called Uber Movement which claims "Let's find smarter ways forward, together" and shares with researchers of an institution the anonymous data gathered over the years around the world to help urban planning; therefore this strategy can be used also in transactional two-sided platforms.

Again, it is important to emphasize the privacy dimension. This mechanism makes sense and has value only if it is compliant with privacy regulations. Data traded must be anonymous, but this is not a value-destroying constraint. Value is embedded into patterns and trends hidden into the data and can be unveiled looking carefully and systematically into this huge and ever-growing data lake.

Merging Client-as-a-Target and Client-as-a-Source Strategies

Enhanced Advertising

How is it possible to get free services? This question, until the early 2000s, was not particularly common, the number of free services being very low. Nowadays, the digital revolution turned this question to be very common, because so many services are delivered completely free. Think about the various social networks, from Facebook to Twitter, from Instagram to TikTok—all these services have millions, in some cases billions, of users, but no one pays to use them.

Don't they need any investment? Don't they pay their employees? The answer is obviously: "Yes." As we mentioned before, there is a very famous antecedent, the ones of newspapers, that introduced the role of advertising. The few euros we (used to) pay for a newspaper are not enough to make it profitable, any more than paying for a subscription to the digital edition. They are a subsidy, a contribution to the sustainability of their business model, which is instead made completely sustainable only by the presence of advertisers.

Newspapers have two customers: readers and advertisers; the former pays for content, the latter pays for attention, in jargon "the eyeballs" of the readers, giving rise to a two-sided orthogonal platform.

As in all two-sided platforms, we have a central company, the newspaper, and two distinct customers: readers and advertisers. We call it orthogonal to underline their differences with the transactional platforms. In this case, indeed, the newspaper does not enable any direct transaction between the readers and advertisers. They do not interact and do not exchange money, goods, or services. In other words, to buy the product advertised by the advertiser, you have to go to a physical store or use another digital platform.

Let's go back to the initial examples now. How can Facebook and other social networks be economically sustainable? The answer is still through a two-sided orthogonal platform model, like newspapers, but their digital nature enables something more.

Let's take Instagram as an example: the popular social network roots its economic sustainability on the use of the advertising mechanism. For a bunch of years, Instagram has been completely free and without any kind of advertising. In 2013, they started adding advertising videos and images in the newsfeed. However, the mechanism on which Instagram is based is not a simple client-as-a-target strategy; it has something more, something different.

Their advertisements are targeted, but not based on the content of the platform in a generic way as it happens on a newspaper. If you sell tennis shoes, for example, you may buy advertising spaces on a sports journal. Still, not all the readers play tennis and part of your advertising effort will be wasted. Instagram, on the contrary, is extremely more specific in selecting the customers to whom to show your advertising campaign, targeting tennis players, tennis fans, and people near to the tennis world.

This is made possible by the data that Instagram can leverage. Our behavior scrolling through the feed, the pages we follow, the content we comment on, the data coming from the apps we have given access to, and many other data can be used to improve the company's ability to profile the users. These data feed an algorithm that allows the platform to personalize the advertising that users see, with the aim of increasing its effectiveness.

In this mechanism, the user has a double role. On the one hand, she is the target of the advertising mechanism, and on the other hand, she is the

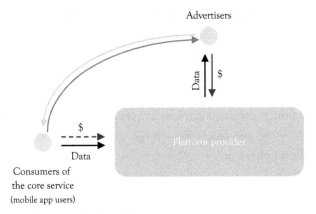

Figure 4.8 Enhanced advertising

main supplier of the information that feeds the algorithm which makes those advertisements more effective.

Thus, the user turns from being the customer who doesn't pay to being the main source of value.

We define this second orthogonal strategy: client-as-a-source.

The double logic client-as-a-target and client-as-a-source gives origin to what in literature is called "enhanced advertising," (Figure 4.8) making the typical mechanism of orthogonal two-sided platforms more effective—especially for the second side.

Instagram didn't invent this mechanism, historically used by Google in its search engine, but it certainly represents one of its greatest examples: we can see the basic strategies of orthogonal two-sided platforms—client-as-a-target and client-as-a-source—build one on top of the other to enhance the value created for the second side and the value captured by the platform, while offering the first side a more targeted advertising message that—at least theoretically—should be a plus for the user as well.

The Genesis of Client-as-a-Source Strategies

Data-Driven Epiphanies

The macro question that sparked the first part of this chapter is: how is it possible to offer digital services for free? And the answer is directly related to orthogonal two-sided platforms. Still, how did companies get there?

Traditionally, business models based on a free-to-the-user strategy are based on the client-as-a-target logic mainly, with the involvement of advertisers as orthogonal actors on the second side. We've seen how digital technologies, smartphones, and the various smart sensors we increasingly use in our daily lives enable a second strategy, called client-as-a-source, which can be divided into three different strategies:

- Enhanced advertising, as in the case of Facebook using data to better target advertising,
- e-ethnography, as in the case of Nike+, which offers data to the parent company to study user behavior with its products and gain insights that allow it, for example, to develop new products,
- Data trading, as in the case of Strava and Strava Metro, which involves the actual sale or exchange of data with third-party players who see clear value in those data

Almost all the cases we analyzed share a common point: they were linear companies offering a successful service (for free) and looking for a way to capture the value they created.

In other words, services such as Nike+, Strava, or even Facebook are born as pure digital services, with only one side: the end-users. In the quest for a sustainable business model, they had a crucial milestone in discovering actors, internal in the case of Nike, external in the case of Strava or Facebook, who see value in the data collected during the provision of the service and were willing to pay to get them. This possibility led to the identification of a second side and therefore to the birth of the two-sided orthogonal platform with a client-as-a-target strategy. In other words, these platforms emerge for a pure business model choice. If you want to provide valuable and (almost) free services, you must find someone paying for them, and unless you find (or are) a philanthropist, you must build a business model to sustain it. Using a by-product of the service provision (data) to make the business model sustainable is nothing more than the logical evolution of the advertising strategies (client-as-a-target) already introduced centuries ago by newspapers.

It is interesting to see how this type of platforms does not suffer from a real chicken-and-egg paradox. While the number of actors on the first side (bikers, runners, and members for the social network) is a value driver for the second side (municipalities, parent company, and advertisers), the opposite is not true. Bikers don't care about how many municipalities are on the other side, as well as runners don't care about how many departments will use their data or social network members don't care about how many advertisers are targeting them (as much they care not to have too many ads, but the number of advertisers is unessential to them). This lack of bidirectionality in the cross-side externality makes it very clear. You can and should start having the first side on board.

This is exactly what Facebook, Nike+, and Strava did at the beginning. The platform approach came only after they developed a successful service for the final users. The tipping point was the moment in which they had a so-called "data-driven epiphany" and saw clearly that another actor was interested and willing to pay for those data that customers left as a "waste" when using the service.

These epiphanies have some implications that we need to consider. First, data have value only if they are collected in substantial quantities, possibly with some heterogeneity in the variables involved (e.g., in the case of Strava, it means having a service spread across many cities) to become a real source of value. This explains why in these seminal cases, the epiphany came after the service's success. To understand to whom the data might be useful, it's useful to already have it.

Second, we need to identify the peculiarities of our data, so we can understand who might be interested in it. Think, for example, of the cases not only of Strava and Nike, but also of Waze and Google Maps. All these apps collect data on movements within cities, but they have implemented different data exploitation strategies, partly because they have different data even though they refer to the same macro type. For example, Strava can also be used by runners, but it is very popular among cyclists, making its data unique and particularly interesting for the transportation departments of various cities.

Another point to consider is the identification of orthogonal actors. Unlike transactional platforms, where the type of actors is somewhat defined in the design of the platform, here we are faced with a more exquisite business logic, in which the platform offers a package of data to potential customers—who will have to be coaxed into buying the service? This dimension also pushes the epiphany dimension of these businesses: having the data in your hands helps you understand who might be interested in it.

A final element to consider is the process for facilitating this epiphany. Looking at the data, we might often come across straightforward assumptions, for example, other actors who are typically part of the value chain of those data, such as bike manufacturers in the case of Strava. But here we must ask ourselves questions: are these data useful for them? What could they learn from these data? More importantly, don't they already have similar data available from their business? Why would they want ours? In answering these questions, we find that the most obvious actors already have data like ours or even collect it themselves; often, the most interesting answer is not so obvious—like transportation departments for Strava. It is difficult to draw a process to identify who sees value in our data—that's why we need an epiphany.

Data-Driven Innovation

If scared by the randomness of the data-driven epiphanies, platform thinkers could just flip the problem upside-down and have a 180° change in the perspective they use to look at data-based platforms.

We saw how Facebook, Nike+, and Strava use enhanced advertising, e-ethnography, and data trading strategies, respectively, in a client-as-a-source perspective and that they were originated by data-driven epiphanies.

Can we completely invert the process? Perhaps starting from those orthogonal players and the data they are looking for?

The answer is yes! It is possible to develop a service not starting from the needs of the users but from the data needed by the orthogonal player—generating what we call "data-driven innovation" (Trabucchi and Buganza 2019).

In other words, instead of finding value in data as a by-product of a service, we can put data at the center and then generate a service to collect it.

This story starts with Jawbone, an American company that launched Up, a very popular smart bracelet at the beginning of the 2010s.

Jawbone Up made a promise like Fitbit: a smart device that aims to observe our behaviors and our movements, to give us various insights about our physical state.

One of the unique features of the Jawbone up, though, was not related to the user's activity during the day, such as counting steps or calories, but during the night.

Did it ever happen to you to sleep only a few hours and wake up refreshed and ready to conquer the world—and other times to sleep 8, 9, or even 10 hours and wake up exhausted and without strength? Yes?

Well, one answer to this very common phenomenon lies in the moment we wake up, or rather the phase of sleep we were in when the alarm clock woke us up!

Based on studies that tell how we micro-move in different phases during a sleep cycle, they developed a smart alarm function. Instead of asking the user what time she wanted to wake up, they asked the user for an acceptable time interval to wake up. As a result, they promised to wake you up during a light sleep phase with the effect of making your day begin in a wonderful and easy way. In other words, they might wake you up 15 minutes earlier, but you would feel better.

In the years of Up's popularity, Jawbone collected amazing quantities of data on how people sleep. They observed the same person sleep many nights in a row and linked these data to external sources. For example, starting from the date and the geographical position, they could get the external weather conditions or, looking at other data from the bracelet, they could get the number of steps, the number of sleeping hours, and so on.

These data are so valuable and so big that in the book *Big Bang Disruption*, authors even hypothesize a correlation between the diffusion of this type of product and the closure of many centers for the study of sleep in the United States.

Back to us—the kick of this story is another app. Not the app that was downloaded to use the bracelet, but the following Up Coffee smartphone application.

Up Coffee is a mobile app released by Jawbone in March 2014. The functioning of the app was simple. Do you want to know how caffeine affects you? Use the app for seven days and inform the app all the times you drink something with caffeine in it (coffee, cappuccino, coke, etc.). In a week, the app will provide your personal relationship with caffeine. How? Mixing these data with those coming from the wristband app: monitoring the sleep, the steps, and so on.

According to Bandar Antabi, head of the special project at Jawbone when Up Coffee was created, "The project started because we happened to be looking at which food items were logged the most often in our food system,"[6] and after an internal hackathon they understood they were missing data.

When and how much caffeine do users consume? To get relevant insights into the relationship between caffeine and sleep patterns, they developed Up Coffee. The data gathered through this app was entered in the Jawbone's database, enhancing the service they offer through the main app and improving the feedback and insights they offer to their end-users through the main wristband app.

It seems we are again in front of an orthogonal two-sided platform: Jawbone creating a platform and one group of customers, represented by the end-users of the mobile app—who receive the main service for free—providing back the data necessary for the service. This is a typical orthogonal platform leveraging a client-as-a-source strategy—much like the Nike+ case.

Still, there is an enormous and very significant difference. There is no need for a data-driven epiphany. The app is generated to get the data and not the other way back.

Similar stories can be told on different cases, such as Parkinson mPower, which seeks to gather data on the evolution of the Parkinson's disease with the double purpose to help the patients in keeping track of their symptoms and gathering data for research. They presented the project with the following words:

mPower is a series of mobile research studies that Sage has run since 2015, culminating in our most recent study "mPower

---

[6] L. Dormehl. 2014. *Coffee App Lets Caffeine Junkies Make Sense of Their Habit.* www.cultofmac.com/287867/jawbone-wants-quantify-caffeine-consumption-habits/.

Progression." Unlike many other conditions, Parkinson's Disease can be uncertain and change over time for each person. mPower allows you to understand your unique story of Parkinson's Disease. Through physical and cognitive activities, symptoms, medication, and trigger tracking, you can learn your symptoms, factors, and how these relate to your medications. These insights allow both you and the Sage Bionetworks team to understand your unique patterns over time. This understanding allows for better conversations with your doctors and caregivers, insight into your day-to-day health and lifestyle, and potential to make a difference in the lives of people who are affected by Parkinson's Disease.[7]

We are looking at cases where a set of data has been gathered for a specific purpose that is not linked to the satisfaction of a need of the users on the first side; in other terms we are in front of services driven by the need of data: this is what we call data-driven innovation.

In other words, an orthogonal two-sided platform can be built not by looking for orthogonal clients once you have the data, but rather by starting from the data you want to get and then creating a service able to create them as a by-product!

The process (Figure 4.9) to follow would be:

1. You need to identify the orthogonal customer: what is the innovation problem? What are the data it needs?
2. You need to identify the data that can solve that problem. How should it be done? What variables do we need to consider?
3. Once we've identified the data, we get to the key point: who can generate those data for us? In other words, who are the users that we will put on the first side and to whom will we offer a digital service through which we will get the data we are looking for?
4. Finally, the trickiest step: what do we need to offer these people to convince them to generate and provide us those data? In other words, what is the service that enables the creation of those data?

---

[7]   https://sagebionetworks.org/research-projects/mpower-researcher-portal/.

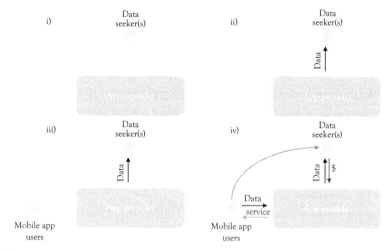

Figure 4.9 *The process of data-driven innovation*

Jawbone answered those questions, understanding that many people are interested in knowing their reaction to caffeine, and then created Up Coffee to give them an answer while collecting exactly the data they were looking for.

To the best of our knowledge, they opened the data-driven innovation era, transforming the data from a by-product that can be used to capture value, to the pivotal point of the whole system—and consequently, the app is now the real by-product!

Data and Privacy

A Rising Dilemma

So far, we've talked about the opportunities related to data and their use to capture value in the platform world.

We focused on the business models and how they work, deferring all thoughts about the social and ethical implications of these business models to a later time. The later time is now, and we will precisely address this topic.

We deliberately chose to start with a description of what these companies have been able to see in the data and how they have been able to ride on these technological opportunities to generate and capture value. These models are not bad and are not good; they are models, they present what can be done relying on data gathered through a smartphone. Still, the usage of those models can be clear to the end-users and therefore more or less ethical. Unfortunately, these models hide quite a few challenges that companies, but also regulators, are still struggling to understand and manage.

The usage of data brought to light questions that were not even conceivable a few years ago. Who is the owner of the data? Who can use it? What can you do with it? Where is the line between what companies do for us and what they do because of our data?

We don't have unequivocal answers to these questions, and we are entering a field where perceptions and regulations change very rapidly. So, we will try to shape the right questions rather than propose answers. We'll try to critically reason about the implications of using data and, as usual, we will start from empirical evidence and cases to do that.

Over the 2010s, a quote, attributed to various members of the tech world, has been circulating on the Web and in the management world that says: "If it's free, you're not the customer, you're the product." A simple, short, and particularly impactful phrase that has two implications: first, the diffusion of a certain awareness on the business model of free services; and second, the emergence of a certain reticence and negativity toward the world of Big—techs and digital companies, often portrayed as unethical and unscrupulous.

This second point soon turned into facts, with real outrages born and spread on the Web—ironically, on social networking platforms. A paramount case is the #LeaveFacebook movement, born after the Cambridge Analytica scandal.

In 2018, Cambridge Analytica, a British data mining and analysis consulting firm, was involved in a major data scandal. According to Facebook analysis, Cambridge Analytica used a personality test to harvest personal data from 87 million Facebook users.

These data were used to generate psychographic user profiles; the information from each profile suggested which type of advertisement could most effectively persuade the users about certain political events. The impact was relatively high. Specifically, the scandal led to Mark Zuckerberg's appearance and testimony in front of the U.S. Congress in April 2018, which was followed by an apology and revision of the Facebook's privacy policy. The dark side of data exploitation has been further analyzed by Carole Cadwalladr, a *Guardian* and *Observer* journalist. She dug into Brexit and gained worldwide popularity with her Ted Talk titled "Facebook's role in Brexit—and the threat to democracy." In relation to the Brexit campaign, she found that Cambridge Analytica's use of dedicated advertisements may have influenced the referendum's vote.[8] She highlighted the ambiguous way in which data gathered through Facebook influenced Brexit's outcome, and, in this relation, emphasized the responsibility of the technology titans in these episodes, which threatened the democracy.

After this scandal, a movement under #LeaveFacebook invited users to leave the platform. The movement made a lot of buzz, all the news talked about it—but if we go to see the number of registered users on Facebook, well, after the Cambridge Analytica scandal, it has continued to grow at the same pace as before (Figure 4.10).

It is crucial to emphasize how this case is completely different from the examples we discussed before about data use. In this case, the data were not used in an aggregated and anonymous way, and, above all, they were used with a particularly subtle purpose related to our psychology.

Still looking at Facebook, in 2020, there was another big public debate about how the platform uses our data and impacts our lives. The debate opened with the release of "The social dilemma," a documentary based on interviews with former employees of tech giants and produced by Netflix—ironically another major digital platform—that shows the darker side of the algorithms used by Facebook and other major platforms such as Instagram or Google. Again, should you be interested in learning more, we encourage you to watch the documentary to reflect on the darker sides of data usage. Nevertheless, despite the huge media coverage, Facebook users did not decrease.

Another particularly interesting case is that of the applications for tracking infections during the Covid-19 pandemic. In many countries, these apps have experienced a real media storm claiming great risks to our privacy.

---

[8] C. Cadwalladr. 2019. *Facebook's Role in Brexit and the Threat to Democracy.* www.ted.com/talks/carole_cadwalladr_facebook_s_role_in_brexit_and_the_ threat_to_democracy.

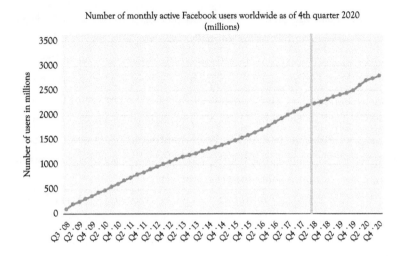

Number of monthly active Facebook users worldwide as of 4th quarter 2020
(millions)

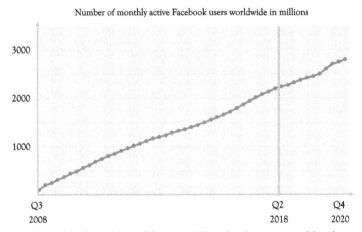

Number of monthly active Facebook users worldwide in millions

Figure 4.10 *Number of monthly active Facebook users worldwide as of fourth quarter 2020*

Source: Statista.

An unusual case is that of Immuni, the Italian app for the tracking of contagion, which has been strongly attacked for the risks related to the use of data. This is particularly surprising as the app was very transparent on the use of data that linked the monitoring directly to the cell phone device, without a connection with the identification data of the user precisely to safeguard privacy. We conducted a study aimed at understanding the determinants of Immuni's failure (Di Marco et al. 2021). The results showed how privacy concerns were among the main factors explaining the decision not to download the application—basically causing the failure of a platform that, being based on clear network effects, needed the greatest possible diffusion.

It is almost incredible to see how all these scandals and discussions happened on social networks that were exactly gathering data about us in the meantime. We are facing a paradoxical situation. Users are increasingly concerned about their online privacy, but meanwhile they generate an impressive amount of data using that very type of service. Moreover, we have thousands of examples of applications that, thanks to the data collected during the service, offer personalized services to their users, which is precisely the key to their success. Think back, for example, to Spotify and Netflix and their algorithms that create personalized playlists or tell how much we will like a movie or TV series.

This has often been described as a trade-off: we give up privacy in exchange for a free service or at least a high degree of personalization. Still, are we really facing a trade-off?

The answer, in our opinion, is no. Why should we, as users, give up the opportunities that data harvesting has offered us in terms of free or personalized services? More importantly, would the world really be willing to go back? Think about how many data-driven digital services we use all the time. At the same time, isn't there a way for companies to capture the value contained in these data, without infringing the privacy of users?

This problem, rather than a trade-off, should be looked as a dilemma: a complex problem whose solution is anything but obvious.

We propose a way to tackle this dilemma, which lies in the concept of business model transparency.

Tackling the Free Services Versus Privacy Dilemma: Business Model Transparency

Our research into the world of platforms and data started between 2012 and 2013; it is not too far ago, but at those times, data usage by digital platforms and people's concern for privacy were completely different.

We can easily think back to one of the first lessons in which we told about client-as-a-source models with the case of Twitter and the creation of the Twitter Political Index based on the sentiment analysis of tweets to try to understand how the American elections between Obama and Romney in 2012 would have gone. It was a communication design classroom, and the face of a girl in the back rows, literally speechless, shocked by the revelation we were making, is still vivid in our minds. We were already used to digital services, giving them—congruently—huge amounts of data, but we were not at all aware of its implications.

A few years later would come Cambridge Analytica, the #LeaveFacebook, and various scandals and movements that created greater awareness, but also a certain distrust of platforms and data use.

And here we are at the paradox: we talked about more and more services to which we give our data, without asking us big questions, ready to enjoy a free service or something perfect for our needs—but, at the same time, an increasingly morbid concern about our privacy.

How can we solve this paradox? How can we make this relationship between users and platforms healthier and more equal?

A possible answer can be found among the first companies we used to explain the two-sided orthogonal platforms and the client-as-a-source logic: Strava. Strava, implementing data trading, created Strava Metro, the service that allows institutions of various kinds to buy packets of data about how users move around a certain geographic area to make decisions about, for example, managing bike lanes.

As with all the cases—not involved in the scandals—that we have discussed, the ability to use anonymized and aggregated data for this purpose is clearly expressed in the privacy policies.

In the days of the Cambridge Analytica scandal, we found a particularly interesting post on Facebook, "Our parents taught us not to sign a contract without reading it, but not to read before tapping on a screen."

In fact, many of us, ourselves included, don't read privacy policies before using a digital service. They're long, often complex, and not easy to find the information we're looking for. This creates a grey area in which many platforms are comfortable: they comply with regulation but leave it unclear to the customer what they can do with the data; they are somewhat opaque. In fact, they even make it difficult to find clear information online about how they use the data and who they give it to.

Strava is not opaque; Strava is a transparent case. Strava Metro is not a hidden service; it is easily found on the Strava website, has its own site, and clearly explains how it uses the data and why.

This observation raised to us a question: what if platforms were totally transparent and explained, succinctly and clearly, to users how and why they use their data?

We have defined the concept of business model transparency as the degree of clarity and transparency with which a user can understand the business model of a digital platform by having simple and clear access to how and why they use the data they collect and with whom it is shared. And we designed an experiment (Trabucchi et al. 2019).

We developed two mock-ups of two digital services. They were trackers like the various Strava or Nike+ we mentioned in the previous sections. The two services had the same functionalities, but simply differ in terms of branding.

For both, we designed two versions. One version is totally transparent, which already in the presentation phase of the service explains that, thanks to the data collected, the service is free and that the data are shared with third-party companies in the transport and medical sectors in a totally anonymous and aggregated way to enable research on where people do sport and how they do sport.

The second version is instead opaque: in the presentation of the service, no information is given about the use of data. Complying with the current law, the information is still available but only in the privacy policy, in the middle of all the other information and with general indications about the kind of companies involved.

We did our experiment by having each participant see two services: one opaque and the other transparent in random order and wondered if and how the potential customer willingness of using the service would have been impacted.

We discovered two particularly interesting things. First, the average intention to use the first service offered to him, whether it is transparent or opaque, does not change. This makes us think that people do not give too much importance to the transparency of data-driven services. As we already saw in the case of Cambridge Analytica, the actual behavior of people does not seem to be affected, and this should suggest to companies that going transparent is not a major threat in terms of user perception (one of the major fears of data-based platform providers). Still, we detected a significant change in those participants who first saw the transparent case and then were proposed an opaque one: their willingness to download the opaque service dramatically dropped. These results suggest that, as people become accustomed to transparency, they might tend to pretend it.

Put another way, we're not used to a particularly high level of transparency in digital services now. So, some people perceive it as a delighter: appreciate it if it's there, but doesn't miss it if absent. Our data, however, suggest that once users become accustomed to transparency, they show dissatisfaction if it is missing. This dynamic is like that described by the Kano's model. Delighters are so appreciated that they soon turn to be must-have for the final customers. Said in another way, what is a delighter (business model transparency) can rapidly become a feature that, if missing, generates huge dissatisfaction—like airbags on a car, for example.

We're not at that level yet, but we may get there soon. If we think about it, not too many years ago, attention to sustainability was in a similar position: a delighter for a few people who paid attention to it back in the 1990s. Today, it's a must-have, influencing the valuation of the entire company.

What if transparency experiences a similar trend? What if it became in a few years a must-have in the digital world? What if business model transparency is the new green?

We'll find out. In the meantime, we can reason about the kind of relationship we want to build with our users on the platform and decide what level of business model transparency we're going to create.

The higher the transparency, the more we can make explicit the presence of the second side to the first and draw potential benefits not only in terms of data-driven innovation, but also in terms of quantity, quality, and variety of data collected.

In the meantime, early evidence on a different approach toward data management is emerging. Consider, for example Doctolib, the French platform founded in 2013 that links doctors and patients. We are clearly dealing with a very sensible field, since it deals with patients' data regarding health-related services; still their approach is clear. In the homepage of the service, just after the main instructional information on what it is and how it works, there is a clear spot saying: "Your Health. Your data." Clicking there, you can find a clear description of how they manage data in an easier and more comprehensible way in comparison to what can be found in the privacy policies.

Platform Thinking World: The MOOC "Exploiting Data Through Platforms"

This chapter lives also as an entire course we developed, produced by METID Politecnico di Milano, and freely available on Coursera; check it out: "Platform Thinking: Exploiting Data Through Platforms" (Figure 4.11).

Figure 4.11 QR code for the platform thinking MOOC "Exploiting Data Through Platforms"

Source: bit.ly/PT_MOOC_3.

CHAPTER 5

Platform Thinking Mindset

Platform Thinking Is a Mindset

In the previous chapters, we proposed a framework (Figure 5.1) to encapsulate all the platform strategies discussed in this book.

We focused on three main strategies to create and capture value within multisided platforms: transactions in transactional two-sided platforms (exploited in Chapter 3) and the client-as-a-source and client-as-a-target strategies in orthogonal two-sided platforms (exploited in Chapter 4). Nevertheless, it is crucial now to refocus on the goal of this book: to rely on platforms as an innovation tool. This means that describing how platforms work and their shapes is needed, but it is not the result. Indeed, in the previous chapters, we have seen in various moments how these three basic strategies can be used in different ways, in different moments of the platform life cycle, and so on, to let the platform evolve toward something different. In some cases, they have been applied working within the same set of players that were within the platform in that moment; in other cases, we have seen that the chance to leverage on one of these strategies brought on board a new side. Now, it is the right moment to summarize

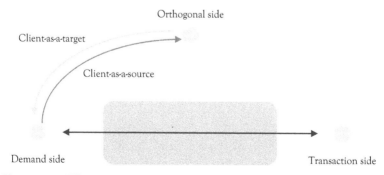

Figure 5.1 The reference framework

all the insights gathered in the previous chapter in an easily understandable, but comprehensive way.

We discovered how platforms could create and capture value through two different strategies. Platforms can sell a matchmaking service through what we call a *transactional* strategy, generating and leveraging cross-side network externalities. At the same time, we have seen how platform can sell the effects of the aggregation of users on one side, to another side, exploiting what we called an *orthogonal* strategy. This kind of strategy differs from the previous one, since it relies only on unidirectional cross-side network externalities and can be translated into two different approaches: client-as-a-target (leveraging the first side's eyeballs) and client-as-a-source (leveraging the first side's ability to generate data).

Notwithstanding, we have also learned that these strategies can take place with different sets of customers. This can happen by *exploiting* sides that are already on the platform, which means that they joined for another reason but now are part of another piece of value creation and capturing, while, in other cases, they can happen through an *extension*, which means enlarging the platform and welcoming a new side to implement that strategy. This creates a 2×2 matrix with 4 different strategies (Figure 5.2):

- *Transactional exploitation*: A new transaction is generated among players already on board the platform.
- *Transactional extension*: A new transaction is generated bringing on board a new side.
- *Orthogonal exploitation*: An orthogonal kind of relationship (client-as-a-target or client-as-a-source) is generated among players already on board the platform.
- *Orthogonal extension*: An orthogonal kind of relationship (client-as-a-target or client-as-a-source) is generated bringing on board a new side.

These strategies represent how to move and what to do to introduce a platform-based innovation. They are a useful way to read what successful companies did and even a possible tool to identify what we might want to do when thinking about our next innovation step in the platform-based world.

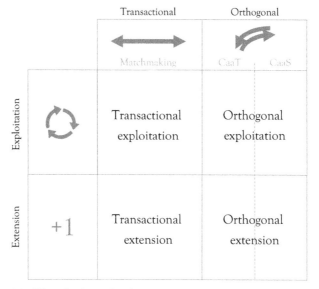

Figure 5.2 The platform thinking matrix

In the previous chapters, various tactics—ways of implementing these strategies—emerged, which can now be positioned within this matrix; let's review all of them, going through the various strategies mentioned earlier (Figure 5.3):

- Transactional exploitation:
  - *Service enlargement*: The platform provider decides to enlarge the services it offers to the sides already in the platform, enabling new possible transactions. This is the case of eBay adding the Buy It Now functions to the original auction service (see Chapter 3).
  - *Platform gemini*: The platform provider decides to enlarge its business by offering a new platform relying on the relationships already established with the existing sides. The new transactions take place on a new platform, meaning a dedicated brand and access. This is the case of Amazon creating and proposing Prime Video as a standalone service (see Chapter 3).

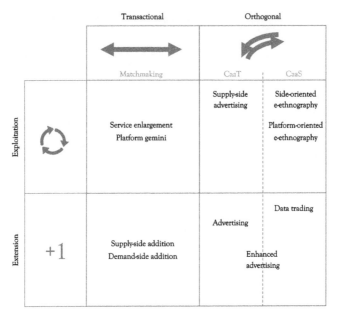

Figure 5.3 The platform thinking matrix with the tactics

- Transactional extension:
  - *Supply-side addition*: The platform provider decides
    to exploit the value embedded on the demand side by
    welcoming on board a new set of customers as a supply side
    that aims to offer something to the demand side, coherent
    with the overall platform proposition. This is the case of
    Airbnb that welcomed on board experience providers with
    Airbnb Experiences (see Chapter 3).
  - *Demand-side addition*: The platform provider decides
    to exploit the value embedded on the supply side by
    welcoming on board a new set of customers as a demand
    side that aims to receive something from the supply side,
    coherent with the overall platform proposition. This is
    the case of Deliveroo that welcomed on board businesses
    creating a line for events and hotels with Deliveroo 4
    Businesses (see Chapter 3).
- Orthogonal exploitation:
  - *Supply-side advertising*: The platform provider decides to
    exploit the matchmaking service happening between two
    transactional sides by adding or offering an additional

service to the supply side through a client-as-a-target strategy. This means that customers on the supply side can pay the platform provider to have a sponsored position while looking for the match with the first side. This is the case of Booking.com that enables hotels to have sponsored positions when travelers look for a specific destination (see Chapter 2).

○ *Side-oriented e-ethnography*: The platform provider decides to exploit the data gathered through the services offered by offering one of the sides an additional value-added service through a client-as-a-source strategy. This means that the customers on one side can enjoy an additional data-driven service discovering something on the behaviors of the other side of the interaction they have with their own products and services. This is the case of Spotify 4 Artists that offers artists to have insights in how listeners enjoy their songs (see Chapter 4).

○ *Platform-oriented e-ethnography*: The platform provider decides to exploit the data gathered through the services offered by relying on them to better understand how customers enjoy its products or services through a client-as-a-source strategy. This means that the organization that runs the platform can enjoy data-driven insights discovering something on end-users' behaviors that may influence how they develop products or services. This is the case of Nike that considers insights coming from Nike+ in their product development process (see Chapter 4).

• Orthogonal extension:
  ○ *Advertising*: The platform provider decides to welcome an orthogonal side to capture the value embedded on the demand side by selling their eyeballs in a client-as-a-target strategy. This is the traditional advertising case that we discussed with the Google (search engine) case or even with the newspapers (see Chapter 2).

  ○ *Enhanced advertising*: The platform provider decides to welcome an orthogonal side to capture the value embedded on the demand side by selling their eyeballs—in a client-as-a-target strategy—while relying on the data gathered during service delivery—also using a client-as-a-source strategy. This is the case of Instagram that relies on data to offer an advertising service to selected eyeballs (see Chapter 4).

  ○ *Data trading*: The platform provider decides to welcome an orthogonal side to capture the value embedded on the data gathered through their service delivery through a client-as-a-source strategy. This is the case of Strava that sells packaged data gathered through their bikers tracking service to municipalities (see Chapter 4).

Nonetheless, we are still missing a point. What is the right new step? How can we understand which of the identified strategies (or of the many we have not identified yet) is the right one?

Data show that making that decision is till now very difficult. In the last decade, countless number of times, a revolutionary startup promised the world to become the new Airbnb or the new Uber in its industry. Some examples? We have heard about Airbnb for cars that wanted to hybridize Uber and Airbnb, Airbnb for pets, or Airbnb for babysitting. Despite the hundreds or thousands of platforms launched around the world, most scientific articles and industry experts are still talking about Airbnb and Uber. One of our research projects (Trabucchi et al. 2021b) started precisely from this observation and from the following obvious question: what makes Airbnb and Uber different from the others? Why are they successful?

What we understood is that being a platform thinker goes beyond knowing the platform concepts and innovation options. It implies having a very specific mindset.

In this chapter, we will present the two main elements of the platform thinking mindset: the idle asset hunting and the evolutionary approach.

Mindset: Idle Asset Hunters

Let's use Uber as the flagship case to go through the most important thing we understood.

The Uber story begins in 2009 in the United States when one of the founders spent $800 for the service of a personal driver. He wondered if there wasn't a cheaper way to get this kind of service, thinking that, basically, anyone with a car and some free time could do that kind of work.

Uber, the service that allows anyone—although not in every country—to become a cab driver and that has revolutionized the world of urban transport, was born from this very simple observation.

The platform was based on the intuition that there is someone looking for a service—the end-user—and that many potential providers might have the time and resources to offer it. Obviously, the number of the potential providers as well as the quality of their provisions depends on the complexity of the job to be done, on required skills, and, finally, on required equipment needed to perform the job. The system can easily work if the service provided is a cab ride; it would be probably unfeasible for a cardiac surgery.

Still, even in the case of cab drives, if the number of potential service providers is huge (anyone with a car and some spare time), without a platform these two parties (end-user and provider) would struggle to find each other. Using the words of Evans and Schmalensee, there is a lot of friction, a clutch in the marketplace. In fact, technically, we talk about platforms as tools that can resolve these market frictions (for any doubts, go back to platforms as matchmakers in Chapter 3).

What should be clear to platform thinkers at this stage of the book is that, once the friction is identified, their job is not over but about to begin.

Uber, in fact, worked to design a complex system that can give value to both parties, to the traveler (e.g., by allowing her to have real-time information on the driver's whereabouts or to pay directly on the app using the credit card) and to the driver (e.g., providing her clients nearby). More importantly, it has managed to bring both types of customers on board and become a giant platform in a short time, overcoming brilliantly the chicken-and-egg paradox and mastering the initial stages of their life cycle. All these aspects deal with how the platform provider creates value and how to reach a relevant position in the market, and we already discussed them in Chapter 3.

In this moment, instead, we will look at what happens after a transactional platform successfully conquers the market. What's next? What is the platform thinker mindset to be developed for the following steps?

Riders   Drivers

Figure 5.4 Uber's evolution: step 1

Uber taught us to overcome the initial stages and get to the point in which cross-side externalities are in place, sustain the business, and the scalability is not the endpoint of a platform, but simply a new beginning (Figure 5.4).

A few years after the launch of Uber, the company realized it had a very efficient platform, but still had several not-exploited resources within it. On the one hand, there were many drivers waiting to receive a call from the app, driving around the city and waiting. On the other hand, a gigantic mass of users who, very often, do not need a ride—but have other kinds of needs. From this simple observation comes the possibility of creating Uber Eats—the service that leverages Uber drivers to deliver food from the restaurants to their homes or offices. Considering the two-sided platform model, they just added another side (restaurants), but what they are doing is unveiling the true meaning of platform thinking.

In the original vision of Uber Eats—and this is still true in some cities—the Uber drivers themselves bring the food to people's homes who at this point will have the opportunity to enjoy two services on the same platform: calling a cab or ordering a pizza.[1]

This new side shows us how a successful platform like Uber has been able to exploit the critical mass created in the first phase of development by going, in fact, to generate a new transaction: the one between users and restaurants, through the same platform (Figure 5.5).

The story of Uber's evolution, however, doesn't end there. What they realized a few years later is that they had in their hands another not exploited asset. Over the course of more than a decade, they collected billions of data points that tell how people—and at this point also things—move around the city.

---

[1] Due to competition from other platforms, such as Deliveroo, and the absence of drivers due to regulations that blocked their operations, in some countries—like Italy—Uber Eats has spread the work of riders later.

Riders

Drivers

Restaurants

Figure 5.5 Uber's evolution: step 2

That's why Uber has created Uber Movement, a service through which researchers, governmental agencies, or anyone with an interest in mobility can access these data and do research on it. This is again a new side added through a new service that allows us to take advantage of a resource generated by the platform over the years: data (Figure 5.6).

The story of Uber Eats and Uber Movement can be explained with what we introduced in the previous chapters. Uber Eats is a typical example of supply-side extension as presented in Chapter 3. Uber Movement is a case of data-driven epiphany as presented in Chapter 4.

Still, what is interesting in the case of Uber is not the application of the single strategies to foster innovation on Uber. If we step back from the specific strategies and look at the whole picture, we may see something much more interesting and relevant.

Let's go back to the first step: the creation of Uber as a service to let anyone be a cab driver. It all starts by identifying the fact that many people have a car that is not being used and some free time—and the fact that these resources could be used to offer a service to someone else.

Third-party research
centers

Riders

Drivers

Restaurants

Figure 5.6 Uber's evolution: step 3

In other words, it starts with the identification of some *idle assets*: time and cars.

Based on these assets, they designed a double value proposition to bring on board not just the end-users who may be interested in the service, but also those who can contribute to its delivery, in this case the drivers.

After having designed, at least from a theoretical point of view, this system, the next step that Uber or any other platform must take is to bring on board these customers, having then the platform finally working. At that point, the Uber story did not finish or stop.

Uber Eats goes through the same cycle: the time of drivers waiting to be called is a new *idle asset*, along with the mass of end-users that do not need to be carried around the city. Getting on board the restaurants is the way to exploit the value of these assets. Still, this requires again the design of a new specific value proposition for the restaurants and to then bring them on board. Uber Movement let repeat the cycle once more; the *idle assets* are represented by the data gathered through the platform over the years of service.

In other words, many platforms believe that the process of creating a successful platform-based service ends once the two sides are on board and generate cross-side network externalities. The hundreds of failed platforms prove instead that this is only the beginning.

When dealing with a platform-based innovation, the most relevant question is not how to build the architecture but what idle assets are not exploited yet and, only at that point, what is the best platform-based value creation/capturing innovation to exploit them.

In other words, it is a never-ending cycle, triggered by a shift in the platform thinkers' mindset: from mere friction fighters—to idle asset hunters (Figure 5.7).

Mindset: Platform Logics Hybridizers

Besides the core concept of idle asset hunter introduced in the previous paragraph, the story of Uber revealed to us a second element of the platform thinker mindset: the attitude to hybridize the platform logic. The same expression, "we want to be the Uber of something," just makes no

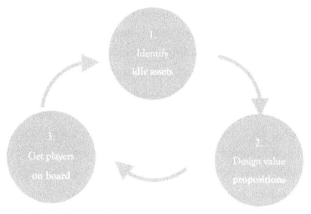

Figure 5.7 The idle asset hunting loop

sense. Uber can combine simultaneously different platform logics (trans-actional, client-as-a-source, and client-as-a-target) to connect different sides of customers and to continuously evolve its platform ecosystem.

To better understand what it means to evolve and hybridize a plat-form, let's have a look at the story of some supersuccessful platforms (Booking.com, The Blond Salad, WhatsApp, and Amazon) and try to read their steps using the platform-based innovation strategies summa-rized in this chapter.

From Transactional Two-Sided Platforms to Platform Thinking

It is 1996, and Geert-Jan Bruinsma came across Hilton.com. It's the dawn of the Internet days, and the famous hotel chain allowed people to book rooms over the Internet in the United States. Geert-Jan was in Amsterdam, and he found out he could not rent rooms there.

He decided to create a website to allow people coming to the Nether-lands to book a hotel room online: Bookings.nl was born.

By 1997, the website was live with 10 hotels, enabling a direct trans-action between travelers and hotels—one of the most famous cases of transactional two-sided platforms in the whole world was born.

The model was very simple: customers booked rooms on the website and directly paid the hotel; the platform kept a percentage transaction fee, which is on average 15 percent globally. This allowed them to scale very fast.

The website started growing significantly, till the early 2000s when Expedia (the U.S.-based competitor, launched in 1996 with a similar value proposition, but a very different operating model since they were buying rooms' availability in advance, as a tour operator) approached the European market. They entered in a negotiation for an acquisition, but after several months, Expedia's board decided not to proceed. In 2005, once Booking was on its way to becoming the European market leader, Priceline Group noticed Booking and bought it for $133 million, integrating it with Active Hotel Limited and bringing Booking.com into their galaxy with similar platforms like Priceline.com, Kayak.com, Rentalcars.com, and Agoda.com. Since that moment, Booking.com has become the main revenue source for the entire holding that in 2018 was rebranded as Booking Holdings. We already saw in Chapter 2 that Booking.com uses a transactional advertising strategy offering hotels the possibility to pay to be more visible on the customer side. Besides that, the company adopted many other strategies throughout its life. In 2018, Rentalcar.com (owned by Booking Holdings) was integrated into Booking.com, giving a chance for travelers to also rent cars.

Challenged by the success of Airbnb, Booking.com even entered in the short-term rental market. In May 2019, they declared that they have more than 5.8 million home-listings around the world, generating 20 percent of the company's overall revenue. Since those days, Booking.com pushed significantly in adding new tools to make property management and search filtering for short-term rentals on their platform easier. The CEO, Glenn Fogel, even mentioned that the future of Booking.com will deal with bookable tours and activities to reaming the worlds' primary travel and accommodation website.

In this direction, aiming to create a seamless experience, they launched in late 2019 a flight product across seven European countries—in partnership with Etraveli, but within the Booking.-com-branded products: the chance to book flights. The evolution continues; now even taxi from airports to the accommodations can be booked through Booking.com. This is platform thinking, but it is not over.

Booking.com is also a great data company that gathered data on worldwide travelers for years. In 2016, they announced Booking.com Analytics and the Opportunity Centre, two services that leverage data to empower property owners to grow their business. The first is a dashboard that features various reports on sales performance, comparison with previous years, with the competitors and so on. The latter can be used to peruse various opportunities and enhance their listings in Booking.com. This continued; for example, in 2021, they released new data to their partners to help them attract more guests as lockdown measures dealing with the Covid-19 pandemic started slowing down (Figure 5.8).

The history of Booking.com shows us what we mean by platform thinking. From a pure transactional platform, it evolved into a multisided and multilogic one (Figure 5.9). They proved to be able to unveil idle assets easily and repeatedly (both in the customers and in the data) and to master both the ecosystem expansion, by adding new sides on many occasions, and data-based logics by looking alternatively at customers as targets or sources. Their trip so far has been inspiring to us, and we know it is not over.

From Orthogonal Two-Sided Platforms to Platform Thinking

The year is 2009 and the place is Italy. Chiara is a second-year student of international law at the Bocconi University in Milan. She is in love with fashion, travel, photography, and is an early adopter of services that, in a couple of years, will shuffle the daily life of billions of people: the social networks. She is active on Flicker and Lookbook.nu, publishing her daily outfits. She likes to share her style with people, mixing and matching brands and clothes according to her own taste—getting a growing number of comments and likes. She is Chiara Ferragni and, in a few years, she will be featured among the most influencing personalities of the fashion world.

With the collaboration of her then-boyfriend Riccardo Pozzoli, she founded "The Blonde Salad." It is a blog built around her interests, where she managed to bring the people that were following her on the various social networks, creating her own personal space.

In early 2010, just a couple of months after the creation of the blog, she received her first invitation to the Milan Fashion Week, making her debut in the "traditional" fashion world.

As it often happens—and not differently from the newspapers we presented in Chapter 2 and the free services presented in

Matrix (rotated diagram):

	Transactional	Orthogonal
Exploitation	Matchmaking — Transactional exploitation (3)	CaaT (1) / CaaS (5) — Orthogonal exploitation (6)
Extension	+1 — Transactional extension (2) (4)	Orthogonal extension

#	Evolution	Idle asset	Platform innovation tactic
1	Possibility to appear before on a query	Travelers eyeballs	Supply-side advertising
2	Rentalcar.com	Travelers planning a full trip (not just sleeping) to a city	Supply-side addition
3	Short-term rental market	Travelers not searching for a hotel room but for short-rentals	Supply-side addition
4	Flights across 7 EU countries (partnership with Etraveli)	Customers on the traveler side who want to fly	Supply-side addition
5	Booking.com analytics	Past performance data collected across years useful for hotels	Side-oriented e-ethnography
6	Opportunity center	Data about what customers are looking for to better shape the hotel offering	Side-oriented e-ethnography

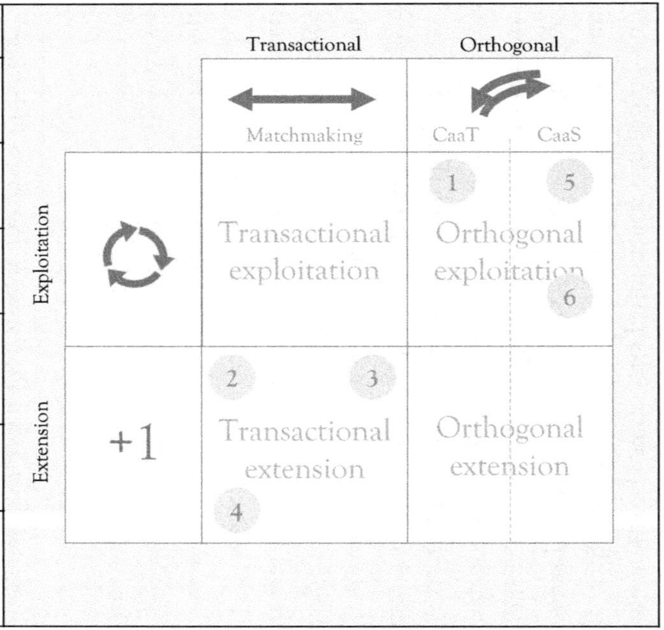

Figure 5.8 Booking.com as idle asset hunter

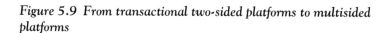

Figure 5.9 From transactional two-sided platforms to multisided platforms

Chapter 4—The Blonde Salad started as just a "one-side" business that had (at that time) nothing to deal with the concept of platforms. Chiara and Riccardo created the content and published it on the blog for her followers. That's it. But, after the Fashion Week, something started to change.

In 2010, brands started proposing business collaborations to Chiara. One of the firsts was Fiat that proposed her to drive their convertible Fiat 500 for six months. Yoox, the French online fashion retailer, bought an advertisement banner on the blog. Many others followed, transforming The Blonde Salad, and more broadly Chiara, in an orthogonal two-sided platform (relying on a classical client-as-a-target strategy).

In March 2011, they founded TBS Crew, the company that will manage The Blonde Salad and, more broadly, Chiara Ferragni as a platform. After getting in touch with some media agencies, some brands started to directly get in contact with Chiara and Riccardo to propose her special collaborations. In those years, e-commerce was rising—and this was a huge opportunity. The collaborations moved from a simple advertising message to product placement—creating content with the brands' products—and then becoming a real intermediary between her followers and the e-commerce website of the brands. This was letting The Blonde Salad evolve from an orthogonal two-sided platform to a multisided platform that incorporates transactional sides also, monetizing through services like RewardStyle that lets bloggers get a fee out of the transactions made through them.

The list of brands working with Chiara increased significantly, from Burberry to Dior; she left the high-fashion industry and entered into more affordable brands like Yamamay. She also started creating capsule collections with the brands, bringing the collaboration further.

Moreover, in 2011, an Italian shoe manufacturing approached Chiara and Riccardo proposing to create a shoe collection with her name. This was the origin of Chiara Ferragni Collection, a brand built on her that over the years expanded from shoes to jewelry, everyday suits, and many other products.

In 2013, the daily visits to the blog started decreasing, while some social platforms became more popular, like Instagram. Chiara jumped on it, bringing her own platform to the Instagram platforms and mirroring—for a certain amount of time—the contents of the blog on the social media. This revitalized the blog as well, while the followers on Instagram started taking off, reaching two million in 2013 and three million in 2014.

In a couple of years, things changed. The Blonde Salad website became an online lifestyle management, while the introduction of stories in Instagram opened new opportunities.

Chiara became a celebrity sharing her lifestyle, her personal life, and her business partnerships with a new tone of voice, entering in the life of people.

In 2021, she had more than 25 million followers, making her and her company a valuable platform that moved from being an orthogonal two-sided platform to a multisided platform that brings together followers, brands, her own products, and many other value flows (Figure 5.10).

The history of Chiara shows us what platform thinking means, starting from an orthogonal two-sided platform, or better—as often happens for this kind of platform—from a digital business without a clear business model that starts leveraging advertising. Using her followers and the media attention, she built a real multisided platforms that generate value for her, for the people that follow her, and also for the many partners that can be pure advertisers, partners for the creation of capsule collections (she even left the fashion world to join brands like Nespresso by Nestlè in the beverage industry or Douglas in the beauty field), or, more simply, transactional platforms that bring her followers to other marketplaces.

From her story emerge some other peculiarities that are worth to be highlighted. She applied platform thinking without building her own digital platform (Figure 5.11). Platform thinking goes beyond the digital services and the ability to manage coding, user interfaces, and data. She relied on other platforms, mainly Instagram, acting for them as a complementor and building her own platform on top of them (see Trabucchi et al. 2021a). Moreover, as we have seen in the Booking.com case, she

#	Evolution	Idle asset	Platform innovation tactic
1	Yoox, Fiat, and others start advertising	The eyeballs of the "The Blonde Salad" community	Advertising
2	Product placement	The eyeballs of the "The Blonde Salad" community	Advertising
3	Intermediary (through RewardStyle)	Followers as potential buyers	Service enlargement
4	Capsule collection	Followers as potential buyers	Service enlargement
5	Chiara Ferragni collection	Followers as potential buyers (for her own collection)	Linear value chain (no platform)

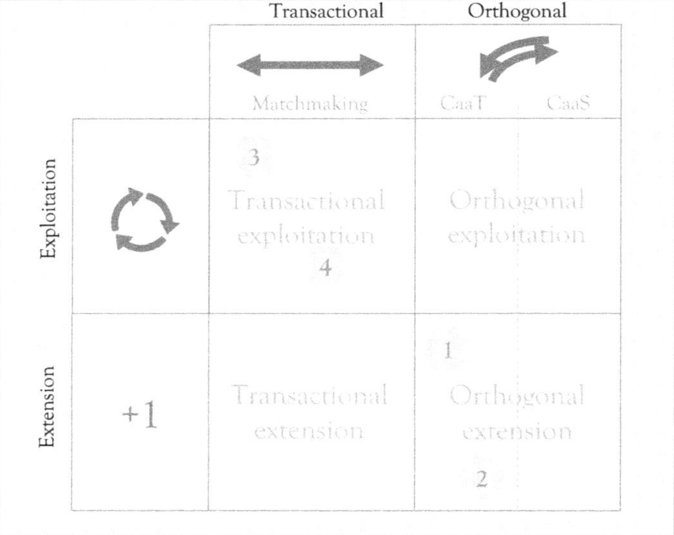

	Transactional		Orthogonal	
	Matchmaking		CaaT	CaaS
Exploitation	Transactional exploitation 3	4	Orthogonal exploitation	
Extension	Transactional extension +1		Orthogonal extension 1 2	

Figure 5.10 Chiara Ferragni as idle asset hunter

Figure 5.11 From orthogonal two-sided platforms to multisided platforms

kept a clear and simple value proposition at the center of the entire system: herself and her life. As she said in the opening quote of the teaching case that analyzes her story at Harvard Business School (Keinan et al. 2015): "For me it was always about sharing my life with people and seeing their reaction to it. That was everything I ever wanted to do."

From Network Businesses to Platform Thinking

It is 2009, California; the Apple App Store is getting more and more space in the business world, while apps are starting to revolutionize the daily life of people.

The main characters of this story are Brian Acton and Jan Koum, who along with Igor Solomennikov, created and launched one of the most famous messaging apps of the world: WhatsApp.

The launch was not easy, with the app often crashing and with very few users, as it was mainly a service that let people update their status (to let people know when users were reachable or busy). Still, in June, after a couple of months from the original release, Apple introduced a new function—a game-changer for this kind of apps: the push notifications. This new feature allows users to be pinged even if they are not actively using the app.

The app evolved, also introducing the messaging component for which it is today well known and successful, and the number of active users increased to 250,000 in a few months. After the official launch on the App Store in November 2009, versions for all the other operating systems were released.

At the beginning, the service was completely free, but the company had a—tiny—variable cost for each user: the cost of the verification texts to activate the profile. It shifted to a paid one; in many countries,

WhatsApp was billed $1 per year, till 2016 when they dropped it off in all the countries.

WhatsApp remained a very simple and useful service, adding features, such as the chance to send pictures and then videos, for years, getting a wider popularity. In 2011, it became one of the top 20 apps in the Apple's U.S. App Store, reaching 200 million active users by February 2013 with only 50 staff members. In 2014, the number of active users doubled to 400 million. Sequoia invested repetitively in the company, bringing its valuation to $1.5 billion in 2013. Indeed, WhatsApp became one of the Unicorns when the club was very small, reaching this evaluation over billion dollars without going public. This is interesting because WhatsApp clearly did not have a sustainable business model, having a very low fee only for certain users in certain countries.

WhatsApp, back then, was not a platform in any of the definitions we gave in this book. Still, it represents a perfect example of network good, which lets us rediscuss the concept of direct network externalities briefly mentioned in Chapter 2.

A network good is a good whose value to one consumer increases the more other consumers use the good. Let's pretend to be Brian and Jan in the days of the creation of WhatsApp. The value of the service is relatively interesting for the two of them: they are working together, and they have an interest in getting together through this service. Still, the service is not as powerful as it is today: they cannot get in touch with anyone else.

Once a third person downloads the app, the game is slightly different. The third person can get in touch with both Brian and Jan, having the double chance to write to someone she would like to get in contact with. A fourth person would now have the chance to get in touch with three different subjects. This effect grows continuously for any new person that adopts the service. This is described by the Metcalfe's law; it is related to the fact that the number of unique possible connections in a network of n nodes can be expressed mathematically as $n*(n-1)/2$. It is powerful if you think back to when the first telephone was introduced. A single telephone is useless, but the value of every telephone increases with the total number of telephones in the network, because the total number of people with whom each user may put and receive calls increases. Likewise, in the case of WhatsApp, the greater the number of service users, the more valuable the service becomes to the community. This links directly with the concept of direct network externalities: the value of the service depends directly on the number of users.

This is different from what we have discussed for transactional two-sided platforms, since in that case, the value for side A depends not on the number of users on the same side but on the numerosity of players on side B and vice versa. Different from two-sided platforms, WhatsApp (in its original version) has only one side of users: the end-users. The service is based on the chance to connect all the users in a network that enables them to communicate. In other words, the value of service depends only on two drivers: (1) the intrinsic characteristics of the service (which means how good it is in terms of technological performances or user experience), and (2) the number of users. The second value driver leads to an exponential growth to this kind of services once the critical mass is reached, generating the so-called bandwagon effect. Similarly, all the social networks—at least in the early days, before moving into more complicated business configurations—are network goods.

This is to say there is a clear and robust rationale to let WhatsApp diffuse for years without a sustainable business model. The more the network enlarges, the more it is valuable.

Indeed, on February 19, 2014, Facebook announced it was acquiring WhatsApp for U.S.$19 billion, its largest acquisition back then. In that moment, it was the largest acquisition of a venture-backed company in history, with Sequoia Capital that received an approximate 5000 percent return on its initial investment.

For years, WhatsApp operations remained stand-alone from Facebook, with new features entering in the service, such as voice calls. Meanwhile the number of customers continued increasing, with 600 million users in August 2014, 700 million in 2015, till the billion was reached in February 2016.

From a platform model perspective, something changed in January 2018: WhatsApp launched WhatsApp Business for small business use, to let organizations get in touch with their customers. This had two implications. The first is related to features; indeed the business version of WhatsApp will get, over the years, various aspects from the end-users one, such as greeting messages, quick replies, or away messages. Second, it transformed WhatsApp from a network business to a transactional two-sided platform.

In January 2021, WhatsApp announced a new privacy policy which users would be forced to accept by February 8, 2021, or stop using the app. This generated a strong reaction by the users, with various millions of users downloading the app offered by the competitors. WhatsApp postponed to May 2021 the new policies but stuck to them. The policy would allow WhatsApp to share data with its parent company, Facebook, generating an evolution in terms of orthogonal platform, becoming a multi-sided platform. The chance to integrate WhatsApp with data usage and the expansion of the business version got along with the declaration of the company to start thinking of ways to charge the usage on the companies' side (Figure 5.12).

From the story of WhatsApp emerges another type of platform thinking approach, starting from a network good (Figure 5.13). As in the case of orthogonal platforms, the initial step (can) looks like a one-sided business and the chance to add new sides represents a value-capturing opportunity. Relying on platform thinking also means to see the network as the basis upon which to build a more complex ecosystem of relationships, with various sides and various value flows.

From Linear Value Chain Businesses to Platform Thinking

For the last shape of the platform thinking approach, let's stay on the West Coast of the United States, in Seattle. It is 1994. Jeff Bezos is there and is ready to change the world. His vision was relatively simple: he was willing to create an easy-to-use retail website with an enormous—potentially complete—catalog of books, literally from A to Z as the logo will show, to be delivered around the states. That was the beginning of one of the largest platforms we know today: Amazon. Its story is long, complicated, and highly interesting, becoming what is known as a "mega-platform" (Kenney et al. 2021); here we'll go through the main steps to analyze its platform thinking evolution.

Interestingly, the initial vision was anything but a platform. Amazon was a brilliant example of innovation, anticipating by a few years the

	Transactional		Orthogonal	
	Matchmaking	CaaT	CaaS	
Exploitation	Transactional exploitation	Orthogonal exploitation		2
Extension	Transactional extension (1)	Orthogonal extension		

+1

#	Evolution	Idle asset	Platform innovation tactic
1	WhatsApp Business	Users as potential clients	Supply-side addition
2	New privacy policy (data shared with Facebook)	Data form users	Platform-oriented e-ethnography

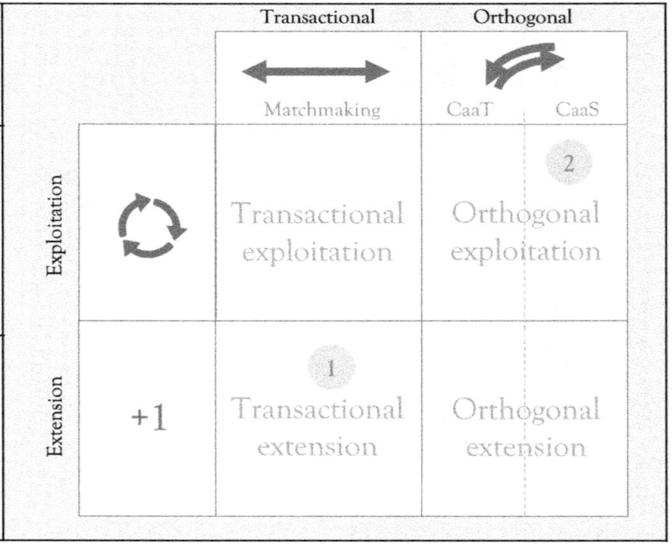

Figure 5.12 WhatsApp as idle asset hunter

Figure 5.13 From network goods to multisided platforms

rise of e-commerce; but it was based on a linear value chain. They had suppliers—publishers—providing them with books. Amazon stored those books in enormous warehouses, from which it could ship the items directly to their customer's doorstep.

The very early signals of a different approach to the business strategy emerged soon, when in 1996 Amazon introduced the Associates Program in 1996: basically any website with a section related to books could link the Amazon site and get a commission for any purchase, creating the seed of an ecosystem. Still, this looks like a partnership approach, rather than an actual platform approach.

Books sales were good, and Bezos saw a great business deal. Why not enlarge the offer? In 1998, they started selling CDs, products like books that would benefit from a large catalog approach. In the same year, the international expansion began, becoming in 1999 the largest bookseller in the United States.

Since the 1990s, Amazon has had insight in the value of data and started working on a recommendation system able to propose to customers the next book or CD to buy. Doing so, they very soon transformed the final client of a linear value chain into a data source.

In those days, in the United States, another company was getting great results, a case we introduced in the previous chapters: eBay. The company was completely different, being asset light and without inventory. This proved to Bezos how also Amazon could be something different. In 1999, Amazon introduced an auction system, transforming the initial linear value chain business in a typical transactional two-sided platform, with buyers and sellers. eBay was stronger; Amazon was not able to profit from this function back then. Still, it was just the beginning of an amazing platform evolutionary journey.

In 2002, Amazon introduced Marketplace, the platform through which anyone can sell goods to Amazon's customers. They started from second-hand goods—and were open to everything. Interestingly, they decided to sell their own products along with the ones of third parties, generating a wide catalog of goods. It grew extensively, reaching 38 percent of all online retail sales.

In the meantime, the innovation evolution of Amazon continued. In 2005, Amazon launched their private label products business, reaching, for example, one-third of all online battery sales in the United States. In the same year, they opened the chance to authors to digitally self-publish and sell their book directly on the marketplace, entering in competition with publishing houses.

Moreover, in 2012, Amazon introduced a B2B sales platform through which manufacturers and wholesalers could sell to retailers and each other.

Among the other expansions, Amazon got prominence with Amazon Prime (the two-day delivery service), enlarging its physical assets like warehouses, long-haul trucks, airplanes, and cargo ships.

All these services, along with the third-party sellers, increased the database of the company that feeds the recommendation algorithms and other internal strategic decisions.

In terms of idle asset exploited, Amazon has a long track record. Among the main lines, we can highlight the Amazon Web Services, launched in 2006, as an external service built on top of their cloud computing infrastructure. Similarly, Amazon Mechanical Turk is a contract labor platform upon which anyone can hire people to undertake micro-tasks that would need human intelligence (such as training artificial intelligence or answering surveys). The story of Amazon can continue for pages, but we will stop here, just mentioning two other streams that are platform related. The first is Prime Video, the on-demand video platform that competes with Netflix, Disney+, and so on. Prime video is a case of Platform gemini, since both end-users and content producers were already in the marketplace (even if doing something different) (Figure 5.14). The second is Twitch, the gaming platform purchased in 2014, which is not mapped since it is a poure acquisition.

Amazon represents a mega-platform, one of the greatest examples in the field of platforms. From a platform thinking perspective, it is a very

#	Evolution	Idle asset	Platform innovation tactic
1	Recommendation system	Customers and products data	Platform-oriented e-ethnography
2	Auction system	Customers as potential buyers for new products	Supply-side addition
3	Marketplace	Customers as potential buyers for new products	Service enlargement
4	Private label	Customers as potential buyers for new products and data about customer preferences	Platform-oriented e-ethnography
5	Self-publishing	Customers as potential buyers for new products	Supply-side addition
6	B2B sales platform	Logistics assets and matchmaking	Supply and demand side addition
7	Amazon Prime	Customers as potential buyers for new services	Service enlargement
8	Amazon Mechanical Turk	Customers as potential buyers for new services	Supply-side addition
9	Prime Video	Customers as potential buyers for new services and established relationship on the supply side	Platform gemini

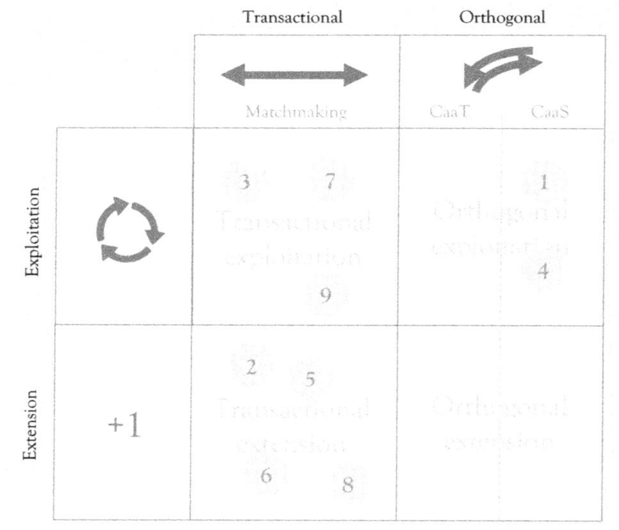

Figure 5.14 Amazon as idle asset hunter

Figure 5.15 From linear value chain organizations to multisided platforms

valuable case that shows how platforms can be built on top of linear value chain businesses (Figure 5.15). This case shows how building on a "traditional" structure, it is possible to build a complex platform with multiple sides and various kinds of value flows. Moreover, probably even more clearly than the previous cases, it shows the idle asset hunting mechanism described at the beginning of this chapter. Amazon was founded more than 25 years ago. It still represents one of the most innovative companies in the world. This is the power of platform thinking applied in a continuous way, year after year.

Reframing

This book is about innovation, and to close this chapter, we need to make some in-depth reflections. When we talk about innovation, there is a single symbol recognized throughout the whole world that appears in people's heads: the light bulb. The closing reflection of this chapter starts there, or rather from its inventor, Thomas Edison.

Thomas Alva Edison was an inventor described as America's greatest inventor. He developed many devices in fields such as electric power generation, mass communication, sound recording, and motion pictures. Still, he is mainly famous for the invention of the early version of the electric light bulb, and for its impacts on the modern industrialized world.

What you may not know is that Edison not only was a great inventor, but also became a great entrepreneur over the years, founding 14 companies including General Electric.

At the end of the 19th century, Edison was working on the Edison Lamp Company and a few years later J. P. Morgan participated in financing Edison's research by merging a series of small companies into the Edison General Electric Company.

Over the years, the name became simply General Electric and the business diversified significantly. GE is one of the first 12 companies to enter the Dow Jones index on the New York Stock Exchange.

The incredible growth of this company caused it to enter many other industries such as aviation, health care, energy, television, manufacturing, and venture capitalism. In all these cases, GE grew primarily through acquisitions, using its financial strength to enter new businesses where the synergy with existing businesses could even be zero.

In its history, GE has been many times the company with the highest market capitalization, most recently in 2005.

Since then, things in the business world have changed though. Or rather, the company's growth has started to take a very different shape. Think about Amazon, described in the previous section. Amazon, in a span of less than 29 years, has gone from being a startup in a garage near Washington to a global supergiant, surpassing Walmart—the greatest American retailer—in 2015 in terms of capitalization.

What's the kick? What is the big difference between GE and Amazon? While both have been able to leverage a financial capacity with few equals, Amazon has been able to put the platform concept at the center of its growth and innovation strategy.

GE was great in growing by expanding in adjacent businesses or even in faraway ones, using some basic assets as a common tool (capital, engineering capabilities, and knowledge of international markets). On the other hand, Amazon transformed all the industries it entered replicating again and again the same basic idea: matching economic actors who wanted to be matched.

CHAPTER 6

The Platform Thinking process

From Reading to Writing: Entering in the New Frame (Platform Thinking in Action)

This is an innovation book, not a strategy book. The point is not to create a new venture to leverage the power of platforms. The point is to conceive platform thinking as a new mindset. In Chapter 1, we discussed the need to reframe our way of seeing the world around us. We talked about the need to create an absorptive capacity to understand the new world we live in—a new world that, looking at the surface, may look like the old one, but after scratching that surface, we discovered how it is deeply different.

We talked about the need to build up our capability of reading the world we are in, to develop the ability to write an innovative future.

This chapter is the turning point between reading and writing.

Chapters 2 to 4 gave the definitions, concepts, and models needed to read the world of platforms. Chapter 5, with the definition of platform thinking and the concept of idle asset hunting, represents the last mile of the reading activity. It deals with the new frame and with the ability to deeply understand the meaning of platforms. Absorbing those concepts represents the transformational step to start writing the future and innovation through platform thinking.

Now we can read and fully understand the world we are living in and the platform potentialities of our (maybe old-fashioned and linear) business. But can we leverage platform thinking in a generative way? How can we foster innovation? What methodologies and tools do we need to design the future of innovation within our organization?

This is what the last chapters are about.

It has been a long journey—for you, reaching this chapter; for us, studying platforms to understand what we are writing in these lines and in the next pages.

Some of the stories you read in the previous chapters are based on existing data; we found them in books or online. The lucky aspect of studying platforms in these days is that everyone talks about platforms. But we knew we had to physically meet platform thinkers to deeply understand their thoughts and find commonalities in their mindsets. We heard many of those stories directly from the words of the founders, managers, and the people working there. We discussed with them what platforms are, how they work, and how they create and capture value. Some of the stories we heard didn't make it in the book, but all those stories taught us to read the world of platforms. And we do hope they had the same effect on you.

We have been looking at platforms from the outside over the last eight years. We have been practicing our ability to read the world platforms, interrogating ourselves about all the digital services we met, used, and enjoyed. Is Google more like Amazon or the *New York Times*? What strategy is Instagram using to generate and capture value? Is Netflix even a platform? You must be born a platform or you can also become one even if you are born as a linear value chain business? And as a network one?

We discussed thousands of hours to give an answer to these and other similar questions, again and again.

Now, the space for stories is over, but our work is not yet done.

This last part of the book is about writing.

You know, we can't write without reading, so we'll be back then. But the goal is different. We want to give you the tools to apply the platform thinking approach within your organizations. Therefore, we'll change the tone. We'll move from the storytelling that characterized the previous chapters, to a more engineering-oriented style. We'll talk about processes and tools. To do so, a couple of remarks are needed.

Processes, as well as the models we presented in the previous chapters, have a clear goal: to manage the complexity of the real world, to smooth it, and to make it easier. Models are not perfect. Processes are neither. What will come after is just an indication. It is the current version of a permanent work in progress approach. Any time we go through it, with students working on it as in a sandbox, or with people looking for innovation path in their organizations, something changes. You can start from here, but consider this a starting point, not the destination.

Second, this process and the related tools are not prescriptive. They are a support, a support for you. If the mere application of tools and processes was enough to create a great platform business, Uber, Airbnb, Amazon, and all the cases mentioned in this book would be ordinary business. We would have no reason to study them nor you to buy this book. The process and tools you'll see next are designed to give a structure to the innovation process by asking you the right questions. The human role behind the process is and will always be the real core asset for successful innovation.

What will come after is made of questions, not answers. You are the one in charge of answering those questions. Be critical on where the process will bring you. Make it coherent with your organization, with your principles and values. And if you wish to know more about the role of criticism in innovation, you should read *Overcrowded* (Verganti 2018), by Roberto Verganti, that surely inspired us deeply in writing this book and proposing this approach to innovation.

Finally, we have been advising companies for years in the field of innovation. Not necessarily talking about platforms, but those experiences in the world of innovation strategies, new meanings, project management, and organizational transformations taught us many things that inspired this process. One insight we had through those experiences needs to be highlighted before moving on. You are not going to transform your organization today with this process. Probably neither this year. This is the first step—the first act you can make to start writing an innovation path. Still, it cannot be the only one. And you cannot be alone. Innovation and transformation require a community, and its engagement is the key to making things really happen. People need to embrace change, need to embrace the reason why change is needed. People need to own it and commit themselves to change. IDeaLs, the research platform where we study the engagement of people in organizational transformation, taught us a lot, and its book (Press et al. 2021) can be a relevant complement to understand how to engage your people and how to manage the process and the tools coming in the next pages.

Getting Ready

Reading, in the world of platform thinking, means being highly aware of the following points:

- "Platform" is a meaningless word per se. Product platform, innovation platform, transactional two-sided platform, orthogonal two-sided platform, and multisided platform tell us much more.
- Designing a platform is not an easy job. Matchmaking can be the starting point, not the arrival one. Multiple value propositions, value drivers, paradoxes, pricing structures, and many more challenges need to be considered and solved.
- Data are not good or bad. Data are opportunities that can be leveraged in the platform world. Keep clearly in mind the value for the parties involved and the ethical principles and laws that guide our professional world.
- Platform thinkers are constant innovators, acting as idle asset hunters to let platforms evolve for what they are: a live complex ecosystem of value relationships that change over time, embracing and welcoming new flows and new sides.

Keeping all of this in mind, we need to switch our mood from the reading to writing. Entering in the world we want to foster innovation in; it may be the organization we work for or the organization we want to create or even the market we want to change.

In the remaining chapter, we will propose a four-step platform innovation process that will support you in reading where you are—through the lenses of a platform thinker—and in designing your innovation journey.

One last note. Chapter 5 showed how fostering platform thinking is an approach that can apply to any kind of business. Being already a platform—transactional or orthogonal—or a network is good, or even a linear value chain. Even though the process that will follow can be applied to all these situations, we'll dedicate more space to the transition from linear value chains to platforms. This is coherent with what we saw in the second chapter. Platform thinking has been developed and evolved mainly in digital startups. It normally recalls, in our mind, startups that became unicorns and then tech giants. Still, the platform concept itself can and should be applied to corporations in any industry, which, unlike startups and digital companies, have huge amounts of assets, history, and knowledge, whose value is potential and untapped.

Even though there is an app for everything, we cannot expect the big challenges of our time like climate change, sustainable living, clean energy provision, or civil rights to be solved by digital companies alone. Uber can reduce the friction between riders and drivers without producing and owning any car, but cars are needed anyway to make this work. We claim the platform approaches can and should also be applied to linear value chain companies producing cars, boats, or bridges and power generation stations.

This book comes from the dream to help these companies to embrace the platform revolution.

Step 1: Step Back and Read (Where You Are)

Innovation deals with novelty, with change, with new perspectives and fresh eyes. The first thing you need to do to foster innovation is to step back.

Whatever your daily job is, your view of the company is biased. It is biased by what you do, by your ideas, and by the history that brought you where you are.

Therefore, to start this innovation journey, you first need to step back and look at your organization, with fresh new eyes (Figure 6.1).

Who are the main players involved? What are the main activities? Where is the competitive advantage? These questions may look easy and obvious about your organization. Probably they are. Still, in most cases, they only look easy and obvious.

You are at the beginning of a long journey. Take your time to assess where you really are, and not just where you pretend to be.

If you are starting from a linear value chain, this step is not related to platforms yet. This step is the foundation of whatever will come after. You just need a way to step back from what you easily see in your organization to have a wider picture.

Step 1: Step back and read (where you are)

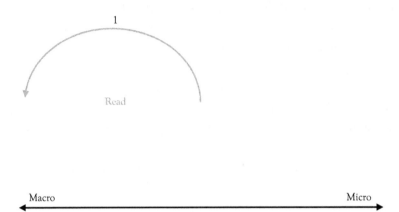

Figure 6.1 Step 1: step back and read (where you are)

Innovation books are full of tools that help people in assessing what organizations do. One of the most popular is the Business Model Canvas (Figure 6.2). It was introduced by Osterwalder and Pigneur in 2009. It is a simple and effective tool to look at your organization and describe it through the answers to nine questions. Answering those questions may be a good starting point to walk back from your usual perspective and take a wider perspective on your organization.

The goal is to reach a value map (Figure 6.3) representing how your organization creates and captures value. There may be various ways of drawing a value map, which also depends on the complexity of the organization you work in. Still, there are new necessary elements:

- A representation of all the key stakeholders involved in the creation and capture of value
- A representation of the main value flows, which can be summarized in terms of
  - Demand
  - Offer

Possibly, money can be added as well.

From this point on, we will be leveraging an example to apply all the steps of the process: the case of a tour operator.

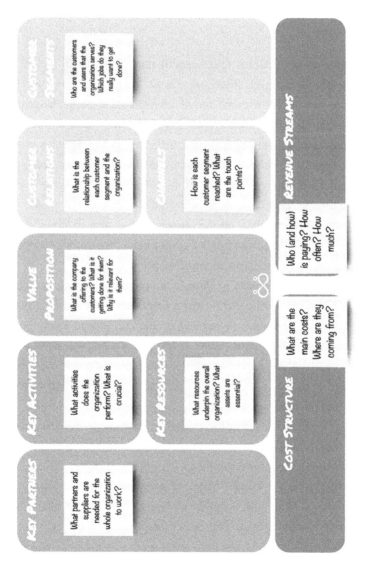

Figure 6.2 The Business Model Canvas (by Osterwalder)

Figure 6.3 The elements of the value map

GreatTravels is a fictional tour operator that specializes in outgoing leisure travel.[1] GreatTravels' head office is in Milan, and it was established in the early 2000s with the aim of offering special foreign language courses held at some relevant universities in the United States, to the Italian academic world, to enhance their travel ethos. The company focuses on leisure travel with substantial investments and considerable development, thanks to the implementation of the concept of tailor-made travel itineraries for the specific needs of individual customers. The project is centered since its foundation on the business-to-business (B2B) market, exclusively retail agencies. The original main product was North America, progressively extended to cover all non-European continents.

The company's mission is to "Create unique travel experiences that will allow travelers to feel better"—travel experiences that broaden one's horizons without prejudice, to respond to the curiosity to know people, the stories and the places related to the journey, and a passion that enriches and makes you happy. Since its launch, the vision that the CEO has pursued is to create and innovate the travel ecosystem that fosters exchange and relationships between all actors involved in the journey.

Even if GreatTravels is constantly growing, they feel the need to create a direct relationship with travelers, renewing and reinforcing their business model through platform thinking.

The current basic system is based on a very simple and traditional business model (Figure 6.4). GreatTravels buy services for a set of suppliers spread all over the world. They may be hotels, experience providers,

---

[1] The case is freely inspired by one of the case studies, which has been adapted to the usage of the tools presented in this chapter. For the original case, please refers to C. Dell'Era, D. Trabucchi, and S. Magistretti. 2021. "Exploiting Incumbents' Potentialities From Linear Value Chains to Multi-Sided Platforms," *Creativity and Innovation Management* 30, no. 1, pp. 31–46.

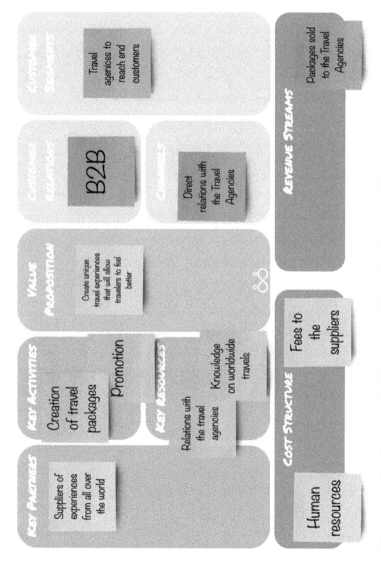

Figure 6.4 The Business Model Canvas of GreatTravels (example)

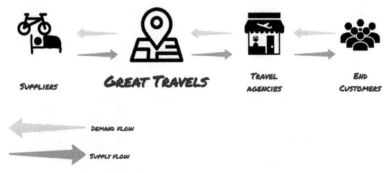

Figure 6.5 The value map of GreatTravels (example)

local guides, and so on. They aggregate these services in special packages and sell them to a network of travel agencies. They manage a long-
standing relationship with the agencies selling them seasonal new packages.
The agencies then sell these packages to the travelers (Figure 6.5).

Step 2: Dive In and Read (What You Have)

Now that you stepped back from your original perspective on your organization, you are ready to start thinking about platforms.

You may have expected to start identifying customers, proposing new
models and value flows with a bunch of players divided into different
types of sides. Instead, now that you have gone beyond the shiny surface
of platforms, you know that identifying possible matches is not enough.
You know that successful platforms do something very different. True
platform thinkers, as we saw in the many successful cases previously analyzed, act as idle asset hunters. That is the point we are making you head
to. You need to again dive into your organization and read it as a platform
thinker would do, looking for idle assets that can be exploited by building
a platform around them (Figure 6.6).

Said in other words, sides, value flows, data, and all the other aspects
that we mentioned in the initial chapters are still not in the game. The
point now is to start from what you discovered in the first step and look at
it with fresh new eyes—those of the platform thinker you are now. This is
the time to go hunting, but you won't be by yourself. We built a tool that
can support you: the Idle Asset Canvas (Figure 6.7).

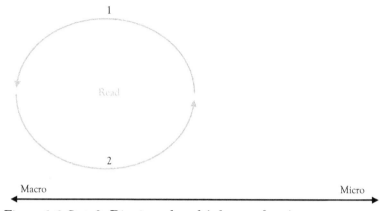

Figure 6.6 *Step 2: Dive in and read (what you have)*

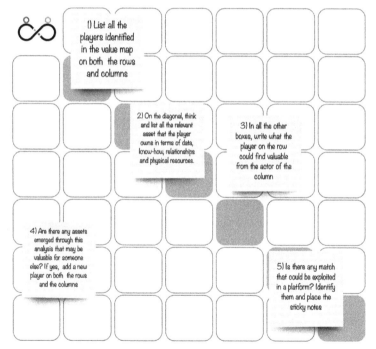

Figure 6.7 *The Idle Asset Canvas*

Think back at the whole organization you wish to innovate. The task now is simple to be explained, but more complicated to be performed.

What's beyond the value map you built? What do the various players bring within the system? Now you need to dive in. You need to zoom in on the details of your organization to assess what assets are available and which of them may be idle!

As we mentioned in the opening of this chapter, this is a support tool. It cannot tell you which are the idle assets, but at least it can support you in identifying the list of assets. Later, we'll try to understand which of them are idle.

So, be ready to list all the players identified in the value maps and to write them both on the rows and on the columns of a matrix. Do not forget the company itself; it should be the first player to be mapped!

At this point, you should:

- For any player (writing on the diagonal), think and list all the relevant assets that the player owns in terms of data, know-how, relationships, and physical resources.
- In all the other boxes, write what the player on the row could find valuable from the actor of the column.

Now stop for a while and look at the matrix. Are there any assets that emerged through this analysis that may be valuable for someone else? If yes, add a new player on both the rows and the columns.

You probably won't fill in all the intersections, but this exercise prompts you to question what the actual assets in the system are and new possible ways of leveraging them.

Let's go on with our examples. GreatTravels starts with travelers, suppliers, and travel agencies. The diagonal reports all the assets we could think of. To name just a few, we can find the offices, the ability to aggregate experiences, the long-lasting relationships with the suppliers and the travel agencies, and the data on supplier performances as the assets that the company itself owns. This is just an example; we thought about assets starting from the categories mentioned earlier (data, know-how, relationships, and physical resources). This should also be added for the other players. The travelers have their time and the willingness to enjoy trips; suppliers have meaningful experiences to be provided and data on the actual customers' satisfaction. Finally, travel agencies have the access to the market and a strong local presence.

Once the diagonal is ready, we can start reasoning on the other boxes. The task is to write what the player on the row could find valuable about the actor of the column. Let's review them, going column after column:

- Travelers may ask for:
  o Personalized packages to the tour operator, instead of standard one.
  o Different services to the suppliers, maybe experiences that are not in the packages.
  o Similarly, ask for ad hoc services to the travel agencies.
- Suppliers may offer experiences not only to GreatTravels (as they are doing), but also directly to the suppliers or the travel agencies.
- The travel agencies can:
  o Offer GreatTravels an access to the end-user's market, as they are doing now.
  o Offer to travelers dedicated travel design, as they probably do.
  o Offer part of their local presence to the suppliers, for example, through advertising.

And now we should stop and stare at the matrix. Is there anything else we have that can be valuable for someone that is not in the system? GreatTravels knows where people will go, and not just where they fly in. This may be interesting to airlines that may better decide their lines. Therefore, we add airlines both as a row and as a column (Figure 6.8).

Please remember that this is a simple example to show you how the tools can support the platform thinking process. Behind each hypothesis, there should be a good reasoning with your collaborators to go in-depth into the asset available in the system and the role that they can play.

At this point, we should go back to the concepts and labels learned in the book and get ready to use sticky notes (Figure 6.9). Identify three colors for the sticky notes, one per strategy; we will be using:

- Transactions
- Client-as-a-target
- Client-as-source

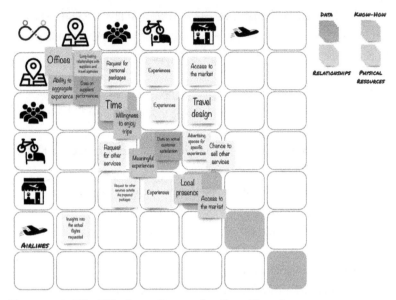

Figure 6.8 The Idle Asset Canvas for GreatTravels

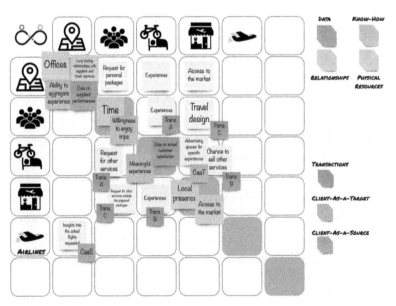

Figure 6.9 The Idle Asset Canvas for GreatTravels with the strategies

The goal now is to identify on the Idle Asset Canvas whether any of the matches pointed out may take place through a platform-based business model. Please note that:

- Not all the boxes will get sticky notes.
- Transaction ones should fit in two symmetric boxes to be reasonable, so we suggest writing letters on them to keep track of the possible matches.

In our example, we can see:

- A possible transaction enabled by GreatTravels among travelers and suppliers (the sticky notes with the A)
- A possible transaction enabled by GreatTravels among suppliers and travel agencies (the sticky notes with the B), which is what they do now in a linear value flow perspective (with no externalities)

Moving to the other colors, we can put a green sticky note between travel agencies and suppliers; it could be a good case of supply-side advertising.

Finally, the chance to add airlines lets us identify a client-as-a-source dynamic, since data could be worked and offered to them by GreatTravels.

Step 3: Dive In and Write (Where You May Go)

You are ready to start writing the future of platforms in your organization. You have all you need. First, your learned how to read the world of platforms, what platforms are, and all that we brought you through in the first chapters of this book. Second, you read your own organization. You are ready to go.

Now, the most important question of all: what are idle assets? Which of these assets have untapped value that could be leveraged by someone inside or outside the organization, via a platform? The advice here is to critically analyze all the identified assets and highlight the potentially idle ones.

We don't have tools to support this. There is only someone that can understand which assets are idle for your organization, for the field you work in: you and your colleagues. Don't forget all that you read before—all the stories we've been through. Those stories can help you see the seeds of innovation, but your critical stance is the real value added.

Once you highlight a set of assets it may be worth working on to foster innovation in your organization, you are ready to enter in the real work of step 3 (Figure 6.10).

This step deals with writing in detail about the asset you plan to exploit through platform thinking and how you plan to do it, with which sides, with which value propositions, and so on. To do this, we developed a support tool that should be used in an iterative way: building the previous, to hypothesize, and then pick the platform ecosystem you wish to build. This is the *Platform Thinking Canvas*, an alive canvas to play the game of platforms, to pick sides, move them, and hypothesize value flows.

The Platform Thinking Canvas (Figure 6.11) is the playground of any platform thinker. It gives you all you need to design—or better, to hypothesize—the platform you wish to build.

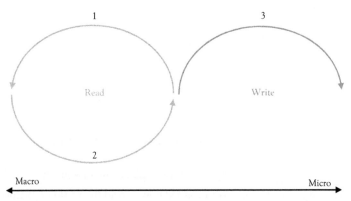

Figure 6.10 *Step 3: dive in and write (where you may go)*

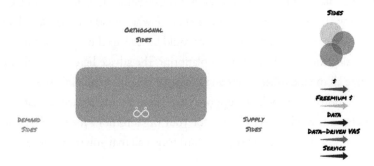

Figure 6.11 **The Platform Thinking Canvas**

The questions are simple. First, who is part of the ecosystem? Second, what kinds of value flows exist with the platforms?

The Idle Asset Canvas should help us make hypotheses first, using all the rows (and therefore the columns) to identify all the sides and the sticky notes to highlight the relationships.

The first question simply led to the identification of three sets of sides:

- *Demand side(s)*: Who is the end-user of the platform? Is there just a set of end-users or more than one?
- *Supply side(s)*: Taking a transactional perspective, who is offering something for the end-users through the platform? Is there just a set of customers on the supply side or more than one?
- *Orthogonal side(s)*: Who is exploiting and gathering value through orthogonal logic? Anyone for a client-as-a-target strategy? Anyone for a client-as-a-source one?

Once the sides are there, the value flows enter in the game. The types of exchanges they can have with the platform are:

- Money (by default or in freemium model)
- Data
- Services
- Data-driven value-added services

Applying this again to the GreatTravels case we would have the following figure, mapping all the players who emerged and all the possible relationships identified through the sticky notes.

The mapping of all the players and relationships would generate a complicated multisided platform (Figure 6.12). Still, this is a dive-in step; we need to enter in the micro-details for all the platform relationships we are hypothesizing. We have three sets of questions we must go through:

1. Is this relationship coherent (and meaningful) in terms of externalities?
    (a) Do all the transactional relationships generate bidirectional cross-side network externalities?
    (b) Do all the orthogonal relationships generate unidirectional cross-side network externalities?

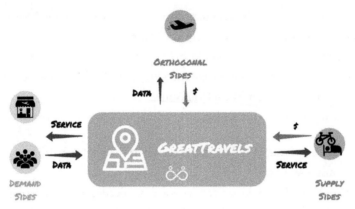

*Figure 6.12 The Platform Thinking Canvas applied to GreatTravels,
first hypothesis*

    (c) Is it true that a growth of players on one side generates higher
value for the other? And vice versa? (If the answer is yes vice versa,
it should be transactional, otherwise orthogonal; if no, then not
a platform).

2. Is this relationship (reasonably) sustainable from an economic perspective?

    (a) Is there an economic value for what I'm analyzing?

    (b) Can the operational costs be lower than the revenues?

3. Should I be the one doing this? Is it meaningful? Does it build on
existing or future competitive advantage?

    (a) Is there someone else that would perform this job significantly
better?

    (b) Is there someone else that is already performing this job signifi-
cantly better?

    (c) Is it coherent with what the organization does?

Answering these questions in the example, we can see how the two
orthogonal logics are not very meaningful. We have those data, but
many other players (such as TripAdvisor) have the same data (they know
where people are located and where they go), and they are much more
detailed. The client-as-a-source relationship suggested with the airlines
is not meaningful. Similarly, we could enable an advertising aiming
suppliers and travel agencies, but the reality is that travel agencies are

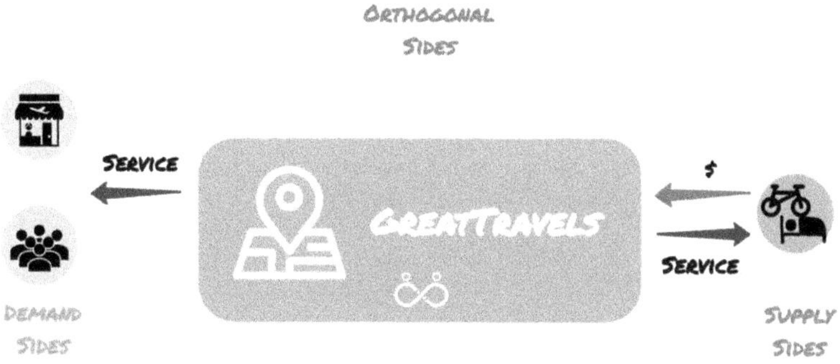

*Figure 6.13 The Platform Thinking Canvas applied to GreatTravels,
second hypothesis*

already full of promotional material from other tour operators, as we
are. Does this make sense? Probably no. This leads to a simpler version
of the previous platform, and we are ready to jump to the next step
(Figure 6.13).

Step 4: Step Back and Write
(The Roadmap to Get There)

You started writing the future of innovation within your organization.
Still, don't run too much. Designing the platform is a needed step, but
you are not there yet.

All the stories we have been through in previous chapters should have
left you a simple, but relevant, message: platforms evolve, continuously,
from something simple to something much more complicated—as we
have seen with the four cases of platform thinking in Chapter 5. The platform you designed is probably complicated; you may reach it one day, but
probably that day is not tomorrow. To get there, you need to step back,
zoom out, and reach a macro-phase again, going on to write the future
path defining the roadmap of your platform evolution Figure 6.14).

We've seen in the previous chapters how launching a platform is
anything but simple, how there are imminent difficulties like the chicken-and-egg paradox, but also interesting possibilities like the evolution
toward a multisided platform. The success of great platforms lies in a
continuous evolution, in the ability to grow and add new sides and new

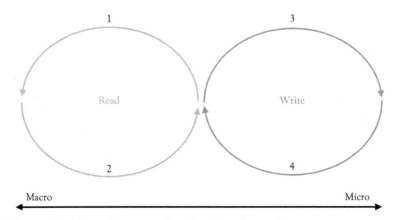

Figure 6.14 Step 4: step back and write (the roadmap to get there)

relationships between sides. To do this, however, we need to think about two elements.

The first is the value proposition of the platform. Adding new sides is an interesting opportunity to maximize the profit of the platform, but it must be done with knowledge. What is the value proposition of the platform as a whole? Giving a clear answer to this question is a necessary condition to create a coherent ecosystem, where the various sides blend naturally. It is fundamental that the platform has one overarching value proposition that sustains all the value propositions and value flows with the various sides. From this point of view, it is nice to quote Airbnb that with its slogan "Belong Anywhere" promotes the local dimension of its global platform, helping travelers to see cities through the eyes of locals, sleep in their homes, and live local experiences thanks to experience providers.

The last step is to define the actual roadmap. Which sides do you start from? Or rather, which side do you start from? How do you bring them on board? How do you solve the chicken-and-egg paradox? And then what other sides do you bring on board?

A great help to answer all these questions is hidden in the previous chapters, but it's important to have a reference map of how we believe our platform can take shape. Trivially, Uber could never have started by creating Uber Movement, ...but we can design a system where the equivalent of Uber Movement will be there and do everything; we can make it a reality as soon as possible.

Let's go back to the GreatTravels example once last time.

The chance to enable a direct transaction between the suppliers and the users is particularly interesting: it can open the organization to the B2C market, after years of operating in the B2B. Still, it has two great challenges. The first one is that it is difficult. They are not a matchmaking company; they are good in creating packages of experiences, not algorithms and transactions based on externalities. Second, this would generate a direct competition with their actual customers, which are the travel agencies.

Probably, starting from there is not meaningful.

On the other hand, starting from an intermediation of the direct transactions between the travel agencies and the suppliers can be interesting. They are already on board, with a similar purpose, in the current business model. It can be an interesting playground to explore the ability and the chance to act as a matchmaker and to get used to the power of externalities. This may be a good step 1 (Figure 6.15).

Once that step is done, GreatTravels may be ready to enlarge its new transactional business to the B2C, with a demand-side extension bringing on board also travelers. This would make the evolution smoother and safer, not only for the company (in terms of activities, skills, and so on), but also for the entire ecosystem upon which its business is based on right now (Figure 6.16).

Figure 6.15 GreatTravels roadmap step 1

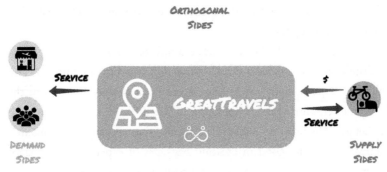

Figure 6.16 GreatTravels roadmap step 2

Looking Forward

The platform thinking process builds these four steps, bringing together two different dynamics: the movement from reading to writing and the shift from a macro to a micro perspective. As said at the beginning of this chapter, this process does not aim to be prescriptive. On the contrary, it aims at stimulating a critical reflection of your organization, while leveraging the concepts absorbed in this book (Figure 6.17).

Before moving on, let us highlight two remarks. First, the process suggested here would benefit a workshop-like environment, getting together the views, perspectives, and attitudes of many people within the same organization. In doing so, it would be interesting to get the insights also

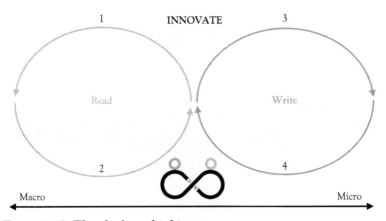

Figure 6.17 The platform thinking process

of external experts that may help reinforce the innovative ideas you are working on. These aspects are out of scope of this book, but there are many innovation management books that could support you in this. Roberto Verganti in his *Design-Driven Innovation* proposes and discusses the role of interpreters, while Jake Knapp and colleagues, in the book *Sprint*, suggest a possible structure where our tools could fit in.

Finally, platform thinking is a never-ending process, where reading and writing should be a continuous cognitive act that will lead the idle asset hunting experience to become an actual mindset and attitude, and not a process applied once in a lifetime—as our logo suggests, with the two head symbolizing the reading and writing attitudes, entering in an infinite loop.

Platform Thinking World: The "Platform Thinking Toolkit" on Miro

This chapter lives also on Miro, the collaborative platform that enables people to collaborate in real time in the digital world. The "platform thinking toolkit," the collection of the tools presented in the chapter, is freely available in the MiroVerse (Figure 6.18), and can enable you to put in place the platform thinking process using our tools.

Figure 6.18 QR *code for the platform thinking toolkit in the MiroVerse*

Source: bit.ly/PT_Toolkit.

CHAPTER 7

What's Next, With Your New Glasses?

What We Still Don't Know About Platforms and Platform Thinking

This book summarizes almost a decade of research, our views, and expertise on the world of platforms. Nevertheless, there is much more to be investigated. We took some research avenues but could not explore all of them. But now, you are a platform thinker, and you may join our quest by taking these topics and thinking about them, or even moving them forward in your organizations.

A noncomprehensive list of topics that are not covered in this book, but still deserve attention in our opinion, is as follows:

- The regulation. The notion of two-sided markets has its roots in the economics and regulatory world, where scholars try to define the kind of markets that seem to have different peculiarities in terms of dominant position, antitrust laws, pricing dynamics, and so on. Over the years, platforms became a dominant and spread business model in many industries, opening the road to other kinds of research. Nevertheless, the role of regulations remains central in the world of platforms. Many of the cases that we mentioned in the book are live or lived relevant dynamics derived from the regulatory world. Just to mention the two flagship cases: Uber operates differently in different countries (i.e., through anyone as a driver in the United States, only with taxi drivers in Ireland, and only with premium service in Italy) due to the different regulatory reactions that different countries have. Similarly, some municipalities created ad hoc laws to limit the impact of Airbnb on hotels or on the neighborhood. Many platforms reached their success entering in market spaces that were not considered by the current regulation, as often happens to deal with innovation. Many researchers and opinion makers talk about the dominant power that platforms are getting—especially talking about giants like Facebook, Apple, Amazon, and Google— seeing platforms as hub companies that are changing market equilibrium (see Iansiti and Lakhani 2017). So far, regulation has reacted to the success of platforms, rather than trying to manage them ex ante as happened with traditional linear value chain firms. This may or may not change in the future, but still it is worth keeping in mind.

How can regulators manage the growth and diffusion of platforms in a sustainable way, promoting innovation?

- Industry dynamics. We mainly discussed company stories in the book. We told many stories of how entrepreneurs found an opportunity on the market and tapped it with a brand-new platform. What we overlooked so far are the implications that a single platform may have on an entire industry. We studied industry dynamics of platforms in a platform-based industry: the one on social networks (Sanasi et al. 2022). There, we saw how the various players tend to coevolve together, absorbing and reinterpreting the innovations introduced by their competitors, and by the new entrants, as would happen in any other industry. There are also emerging insights into the change that platforms can bring in the entire value chain of pre-existing industries. Two examples? The music and the television industry. After the rise of iTunes and Spotify, the music industry changed significantly. The music majors, known as the Big Six, merged and remained just three. The three of them went through an important organizational restructuring becoming "entertaining companies," enlarging the skills they leverage on and developing new ways to discover talents, develop music, and launch music (Trabucchi et al. 2017). Two concrete and simple changes of the change driven by Spotify? Songs' length shortened[1]—due to how music consumption is paid to artists in platforms like Spotify—and the structure of commercial songs changed, to increase the likelihood to be listed till the 30th second, when the stream is paid.[2] Similarly, Netflix and Co. pushed all the traditional television broadcasters to react. While the traditional channels' viewers decrease constantly,[3] almost any broadcaster joins the platform competition with their own platforms.

How can established companies move from reaction to their industry dynamics to innovators in platform-driven industry dynamics?

- Value sharing. The phenomena linked to digital platforms are rapidly crossing the boundaries of single businesses and are beginning to become relevant to the dynamics of markets, global economies, and, ultimately, the social and political dynamics of our planet. Those same technologies that promised to make business more democratic by allowing small producers to access the global market or by enabling interesting and virtuous phenomena such as the sharing economy are now threatening to make the world an oligopoly. A solution typically called winner-takes-all is taking shape in which a small number of "hub companies"—including Alibaba, Alphabet/Google, Amazon, Apple, Baidu, Facebook, Microsoft, and Tencent—occupy the central positions.

---

[1] M. Zachary. 2019. *How Streaming Affects the Lengths of Songs*, www.theverge .com/2019/5/28/18642978/music-streaming-spotify-song-length-distribution-production-switched-on-pop-vergecast-interview.

[2] *Streaming Royalties Are Changing How Popular Songs Are Made.* https:// plainenglish.com/lessons/streaming-royalties-are-changing-how-popular-songs-are-made/.

[3] P. Lee. 2022. *Traditional TV Wanes: Television Is About to Dip Below Half of All UK Video Viewing.* www2.deloitte.com/uk/en/insights/industry/technology/technology-media-and-telecom-predictions/2022/tv-viewership-decline.html.

Undoubtedly, these companies create real and effective value for customers, but, on the other hand, they capture a (maybe) too huge and ever-growing share of this value.

Iansiti and Lakhani already in 2017 introduced the concepts of *hub* company and domino effect.

They build on Albert-László Barabási effect that makes it possible to predict that the evolution of the digital network will naturally lead to the emergence of positive feedback loops that create increasingly large, important, and highly connected hubs. Once a hub is highly connected in one sector of the economy (such as mobile telecommunications), it will enjoy a crucial advantage when it starts connecting in a new sector (e.g., automobiles), creating a kind of digital domino effect that will most likely lead toward an oligopoly. Hub companies are creating a new, nonconventional way to compete. They don't win on the market because they invest in the development of new products with better functionalities or lower prices.

On the contrary, they enter other industries by exploiting previously generated impressive network factors and transforming the competition from product driven to network driven. However, it is now considered inevitable that the hub company should be an active partner in solving the negative sides that they are generating. There is a real possibility that, in a short period of time, hub companies will really drive our economy. This will require them to fully consider the long-term impact of their decisions on society, to prioritize the large economic ecosystems that increasingly revolve around them, and to accept their ethical responsibilities. There is a growing demand for these companies to add a value-sharing dimension to their traditional value creation and value capturing. The ability to build and maintain a healthy ecosystem is more relevant in the long run than the ability to attack and conquer entire industries.

As an important closing note, there are also emerging companies, like DataSwift, which are building their entire value proposition on giving back the power to the users. DataSwift claims to "unlock the value of data" creating the opportunity to directly monetize data for the data creator. This can be the sign of a different way to share value, but the question for us remains: How can we—not only as managers, but also as users—drive the conscious and sustainable evolution of platform companies?

- B2B platforms, sustainability, grand challenges, and much more: Most cases presented in this book deal with platforms that, at least on one of the sides, have end-users, consumers. The early days of the platform research taught us that the scale is, at the same time, one of the greatest opportunities and one of the peculiarities of platforms that can lead to situations where "winner-takes-all" or eventually "winders-take-all," showing the benefit of having big platforms. Dealing with consumers surely favors the scale. Nevertheless, there are many cases of successful B2B2B platforms, moving from Amazon Business to many other smaller and more industry-related fields. This book, though, was not meant to introduce omni-comprehensive stories, but to show a mindset: a mindset that goes beyond scales and consumers; a mindset that deals with the chance to create and capture value in a diffused way; a mindset that is highly coherent with many fields that are different from those emerging from the average success story told in this book. Industrial relations, supply chains, and, more broadly, the B2B world can see in this mindset great opportunities and potentialities to explore. Don't get us wrong. Many cases exist, but we believe that much more innovation can be fostered there. Similarly, platforms are a model that can enhance sustainable oriented models, peer productions, share-based models, and more broadly the ability of the society to tackle some of the grand challenges we are going through. We do hope that platform thinking may help established organizations and associations in these fields to consider platforms as a valuable model upon which to rely to foster innovation and generate a greater impact on our society.

- Emerging technologies. In 2008, Satoshi Nakamoto, a programmer whose real identity is still unknown, published the white paper "Bitcoin: a peer-to-peer electronic cash system," explaining the idea of peer-to-peer virtual currencies, able to operate worldwide without the use of financial intermediaries: "The Bitcoin protocol." The central idea was to allow people to use money in a decentralized way, without being tied to any institution, or without the need for permissions. It was a major statement of protest toward the financial industry, which had caused the biggest economic crisis since the Great Depression. Ten years later, its most important incarnation, Bitcoin, had reached a market capitalization of $830+ billion and, together with hundreds of other cryptocurrencies, the idea had lost its anticonformist/antiestablishment message. This technology is showing that there is a different way to create platforms. Many of the startups that are now relying on this technology seem to put the idea of value sharing at the heart of the project. At the same time, many of the drivers that we have seen in the book as crucial for a platform development—such as trust building—are, in this case, embedded in the technical features of the technology itself. This is letting emerge blockchain-based decentralized platforms that look slightly different from what we are most familiar with as users, but the very technology they are based on—with the values of transparency and sharing at the core—could foster the emergence of new businesses and new business models where the value of the data generated during the service will also be shared with users—a technology to consider when evaluating the creation of a new platform (see Trabucchi et al. 2020). Blockchain is an example; other technologies may provide similar changes in the world of platforms. We may lay out similar reasoning on Web 3, the metaverse, generative AI and many others.

How can emerging technologies let evolve platform models, by exploiting the mindset of a platform thinker?

- All that glitters is not gold. We want to close this list with a little clarification. This book is positive about platforms. We aimed to show the bright side of a business structure that—in our opinion—can and should help established companies, innovators, and entrepreneurs to create and capture value in new ways that are unlocked by the power of platforms if contraposed to traditional linear value chain mechanisms. Nevertheless, besides the bright side, there is, clearly, a dark side. We do believe that a platform model cannot be good or bad per se; it is the organization that stays behind the platform that can make it good or bad, and what we have tried to highlight here are mainly the potentialities and opportunities offered by these models. You, as an innovator, are in charge to make a proper use of these models, being aware that many scandals, phenomena, or more broadly events have showed how platforms can have various downsides. We previously mentioned all the privacy-related issues, focusing on data usage, but there are many other phenomena that have been widely addressed by other authors. Haidt (2022) highlights many deviations of the platform world that took place in the last decade, moving from fake news and videos to the threat to democracy. Others criticized the gigantic amount of investments done in companies that could not generate profit, but often burn money for years (Tully 2019). Or again, the threat that some of these enormous platforms can make to the democracy, bringing us to the so-called "age of surveillance capitalism" (Zuboff 2019). These are just a few references to explore the whole world that we briefly mentioned in this book, but worth exploring to have a 360° view on the platforms' world.

Closing the Loop

It has been a long journey, and we are almost nearing the destination. Do you recall where we started from? We just landed in Rome and took a taxi to reach a client…and we met a taxi driver. The taxi driver was in love with Airbnb but hated Uber, without seeing the strong connection among the two.

We used that example to explain why, in our humble opinion, "another book on platforms" was necessary because this is an innovation book meant to help professionals in seeing the innovation power behind platforms.

We wrote with the aim to provide the absorptive capacity needed to understand current platforms and their trajectories fully. Then, we proposed a concrete process and tools to put your existing business at the beginning of these trajectories and imagine a roadmap to transform it into a platform-based business.

Now you should be there. You should be able to walk around the city, or probably to surf around the digital world with your smartphone, and see platforms where you used to see just services. Thanks to your new glasses, you should be able to see customers where you used to see suppliers, you should be able to see the reason why something is free, or, simply, you should be able to understand something more on why digital services evolve, change, and get on board different sides.

Still, this is not all you should see. You should be able to see something more. You should be able to see opportunities hidden within the organizations you work in, no matter whether that's a platform, a traditional linear value chain company that was always thought to be as far as possible from the platform world, or one of those companies that were forced to move toward platforms. Your brand-new platform glasses should let you see that wherever you are, whatever you are doing, there must be somewhere an idle asset that can nurture the platform-driven innovation. Those idle assets can be, with the tools you found here, the raw material to write the future of platforms, as we promised at the beginning of the book.

We may close it here. Wish you the best of luck with your innovation journey and hope that what you got here will help you innovate your professional world.

Before that, though, we would like to ask you one last question: What should come with you, and what may you leave behind?

This book is full of examples. It is a book full of stories that tell the actions of those who helped craft the world of platforms. These stories taught us almost all we know on the world of platforms. We used them for a very simple reason: we are human beings. And, as human beings, we learn through stories; that's what we have done since we were kids. Stories are what we remember and what let us remember things.

Notwithstanding this being an innovation book, these books have a curse that cannot be avoided. Innovation books get old very quickly. Or better, innovations, especially in the digital world, become old in a very short amount of time. Many of the examples, extensions, evolutions, and nuances that we captured in this book will be old before you read these lines. Many—we hope all—of the companies we mentioned here will have added new services, dismissed some of those we mentioned, rebranded, merged with other platforms, and so on when you will be reading this book—no matter whether you read it fresh out of the press or years after.

A couple of years ago, we read the book *The Airbnb story* by Leigh Gallagher. At the very beginning, the author reports a conversation between Brian Chesky (one of the Airbnb founders) and herself regarding her willingness to write a book on the platform. He said:

> The problem with a book is that it's a fixed imprint of a company at a particular moment in time. I'm thirty-four. Our company is young. We're going to go on to do many more things from here. Where everyone thinks Airbnb is today, is where we were two years ago. (Gallagher 2017)

She wrote the book (it is a great book, we loved it!) and it had a great success, taking a snapshot of what brought Airbnb there.

Our book is slightly different, though. We were not aiming to tell a story. We aimed to show you something, something that lies behind the stories we told. We are talking about the models we presented. They don't get old that fast. The distance between Google and a newspaper is much less than many of us can expect. Platforms providers adapted and smoothed logic and dynamics that have been in the business world for a while and will be for some more time again. Leave behind the stories and focus on what can help you read the stories of the companies that are exploring the world of platform now, while you are reading this book.

The Platform Thinking Ecosystem

"Platform thinking" is the keystone of an ecosystem that we built over the last decade of research that resulted in 25 published papers in academic peer-reviewed journals. The papers represent our starting point, of a whole world of projects that took place over the last years and will continue to grow in the next. The whole project we built so far is briefly outlined here. On **platformthinking.eu**, you can find all the updates on our project and its future extensions. The fil rouge that links all the projects is the logo introduced in Chapter 6: the infinite loop that can be read as a representation of a transactional two-sided platform, where the two heads represent the two sides, and the two dots in the flow the matching that the platform enables. At the same time, you can see two shaking hands stylized in the logo as well as two people, putting at the center the human side that we want to highlight with platform thinking.

Platform Thinking

Building on our research, we developed many complementary projects with two different goals: teaching and disseminating.

We teach "platform thinking" in various courses at Politecnico di Milano, our home university, and in many other universities where we have strong research relationships, such as Trinity College Dublin, or Toulouse Business School.

On top of teaching, we have built numerous projects, to disseminate our research and our view of the platform world, that are complementary to the book:

- *MOOCs "Platform Thinking"*: We recorded three massive online open courses (MOOCS; "Platform Thinking: what's beyond Uber?," "Platform Thinking: designing a platform," and "Platform Thinking: exploiting data through platforms") that are available on **Coursera** (bit.ly/PT_Coursera) before writing this book. A fourth one followed: "Platform Thinking 4 the Metaverse." They are produced within the *Polimi Open Knowledge* project by METID Politecnico di Milano.

Platform Thinking MOOCs on Coursera

- *The podcast "Talking about platforms"*: In any episode, with Philip Meier, see the presentation of an academic paper by leading scholars, discussing its practical implications. It is available on the major podcasting platforms like *Spotify* and *Apple Podcasts* (bit.ly/PT_TAP).

Talking about platforms

- *Miro templates*: We have distributed the Miro version of the templates we created for the platform thinking process. They are freely featured in the *Miro* within the *MiroVerse* (the Miro community templates gallery) and freely available for anyone who uses Miro (bit.ly/PT_Toolkit).

Platform thinking toolkit in the MiroVerse

Building on this experience, we also created a revised version of the Business Model Canvas and the Lean Canvas that considers the peculiarities of platforms. This is the Platform Thinking Business Model Canvas, that is as well available for free with dedicated instructions in the Miroverse (bit.ly/PT_PlatformCanvas).

Platform thinking business model canvas in the MiroVerse

- *"The Platform Room"*: We do believe in the power of dissemination of scientific knowledge. Therefore, we scripted—and recorded—short videos that aim to make all our scientific papers in the field of platforms understandable and accessible to a wider audience. They are available on our YouTube channels, more episodes to come (bit.ly/PT_ PlatformRoom).

The Platform Room

- *Symplatform*: We founded (along with Laurent Muzellec from Trinity College Dublin and Sébastien Ronteau from Audencia) an annual international conference on digital platforms that aims to bring at the same table professionals and academics interested in the world of platforms. The first edition took place in July 2020, the second in May 2021, and the third in April 2022. More to come. Further info at https://symplatform.com.

Symplatform

References

Chapter 1

Baricco, A. 2018. *The Game*. Torino: Einaudi.

Buganza, T., C. Dell'Era, E. Pellizzoni, D. Trabucchi, and R. Verganti. 2015. "Unveiling the Potentialities Provided by New Technologies: A Process to Pursue Technology Epiphanies in the Smartphone App Industry." *Creativity and Innovation Management* 24, no. 3, pp. 391–414.

Cohen, W.M. and D.A. Levinthal. 1990. "Absorptive Capacity: A New Perspective on Learning and Innovation." *Administrative Science Quarterly* 35, no. 1, pp. 128–152.

Fidler, R.F. 1997. *Mediamorphosis: Understanding New Media*. New York, NY: Pine Forge Press.

Moore, G. 2008. *Dealing With Darwin: How Great Companies Innovate at Every Phase of Their Evolution*. New York, NY: Wiley.

Rogers, E. 2003. *Diffusion of Innovations*. New York, NY: Simon and Schuster.

Trabucchi, D., L. Talenti, and T. Buganza. 2019. "How Do Big Bang Disruptors Look Like? A Business Model Perspective." *Technological Forecasting and Social Change* 141, pp. 330–340.

Verganti, R. 2009. *Design Driven Innovation: Changing the Rules of Competition by Radically Innovating What Things Mean*. Boston: Harvard Business Press.

Chapter 2

Gawer, A. and M.A. Cusumano. 2014. "Industry Platforms and Ecosystem Innovation." *Journal of Product Innovation Management* 31, no. 3, pp. 417–433.

Luchetta, G. 2014. "Is the Google Platform a Two-Sided Market?." *Journal of Competition Law and Economics* 10, no. 1, pp. 185–207.

Meyer, M.H. and A.P. Lehnerd. 1997. *The Power of Product Platforms*. New York, NY: Simon and Schuster.

Rochet, J.C. and J. Tirole. 2003. "Platform Competition in Two-Sided Markets." *Journal of the European Economic Association* 1, no. 4, pp. 990–1029.

Sanderson, S. and M. Uzumeri. 1995. "Managing Product Families: The Case of the Sony Walkman." *Research Policy* 24, no. 5, pp. 761–782.

Trabucchi, D. and T. Buganza. 2022. "Landlords With No Lands: A Systematic Literature Review on Hybrid Multi-Sided Platforms and Platform Thinking." *European Journal of Innovation Management* 25, no. 6, pp. 64–96.

Chapter 3

Evans, D.S. and R. Schmalensee. 2016. *Matchmakers: The New Economics of Multi-Sided Platforms*. Boston: Harvard Business Review Press.

Parker, G.G. and M.W. Van Alstyne. 2005. "Two-Sided Network Effects: A Theory of Information Product Design." *Management Science* 51, no. 10, pp. 1494–1504.

Rifkin, J. 2014. *The Zero Marginal Cost Society: The Internet of Things, the Collaborative Commons, and the Eclipse of Capitalism*. New York, NY: St. Martin's Press.

Saxena, D., L. Muzellec, and D. Trabucchi. 2020. "BlaBlaCar: Value Creation on a Digital Platform." *Journal of Information Technology Teaching Cases* 10, no. 2, pp. 119–126.

Trabucchi, D. 2020. "Let's Get a Two-Sided Platform Started: Tactics to Solve the Chicken and Egg Paradox." *Journal of Business Ecosystems (JBE)* 1, no. 1, pp. 63–77.

Trabucchi, D. and T. Buganza. 2020. "Fostering Digital Platform Innovation: From Two to Multi-Sided Platforms." *Creativity and Innovation Management* 29, no. 2, pp. 345–358.

Trabucchi, D. and T. Buganza. 2021. "Entrepreneurial Dynamics in Two-Sided Platforms: the Influence of Sides in the Case of Friendz." *International Journal of Entrepreneurial Behavior and Research*.

Trabucchi, D., T. Buganza, and R. Verganti. 2021a. "Quantity or Quality? Value Creation in Two-Sided Platforms." *Technology Analysis & Strategic Management* 33, no. 2, pp. 162–175.

Trabucchi, D., L. Muzellec, S. Ronteau, and T. Buganza. 2021b. "The Platforms' DNA: Drivers of Value Creation in Digital Two-Sided Platforms." *Technology Analysis and Strategic Management*, pp. 1–14.

Trabucchi, D., L. Gastaldi, E. Pellizzoni, T. Buganza, and M. Corso. 2018. "Launching a Two-Sided Platform: The Role of Platform Enhancers." In *R&D Management Conference*, pp. 1–12.

Trischler, M., P. Meier, and D. Trabucchi. 2021. "Digital Platform Tactics: How to Implement Platform Strategy Over Time." *Journal of Business Models* 9, no. 1, pp. 67–76.

Williamson, O.E. 1979. "Transaction-Cost Economics: The Governance of Contractual Relations." *The Journal of Law and Economics* 22, no. 2, pp. 233–261.

Chapter 4

Buganza, T., D. Trabucchi, and E. Pellizzoni. 2020. "Limitless Personalization: The Role of Big Data in Unveiling Service Opportunities." *Technology Analysis and Strategic Management* 32, no. 1, pp. 58–70.

Di Marco, D., D. Trabucchi, T. Buganza, and R. Verganti. 2021. "It's Not UBER: How the Adoption of COVID-19 Contact Tracing Apps Work Using an Amended Model Based on the UTAUT perspective." In *IPDMC 2021*, pp. 1–15.

Trabucchi, D. and T. Buganza. 2019. "Data-Driven Innovation: Switching the Perspective on Big Data." *European Journal of Innovation Management* 22, no. 1, pp. 3–40.

Trabucchi, D., T. Buganza, and A.S. Patrucco. 2019. "Do You Care How Digital Platforms Use Your Data? The Role of Transparency in Data-Driven Business Models." In *R&D Management Conference*, pp. 1–15.

Trabucchi, D., T. Buganza, and E. Pellizzoni. 2017. "Give Away Your Digital Services: Leveraging Big Data to Capture Value." *Research-Technology Management* 60, no. 2, pp. 43–52.

Chapter 5

Keinan, A., K. Maslauskaite, S. Crener, and V. Dessain. 2015. *The Blonde Salad.* Boston: Harvard Business Publishing.

Kenney, M., D. Bearson, and J. Zysman. 2021. "The Platform Economy Matures Measuring Pervasiveness and Exploring Power." *Socio-Economic Review* 19, no. 4, pp. 1451–1483.

Trabucchi, D., T. Buganza, L. Muzellec, and S. Ronteau. 2021a. "Platform-Driven Innovation: Unveiling Research and Business Opportunities." *Creativity and Innovation Management* 30, no. 1, pp. 6–11.

Trabucchi, D., S. Sanasi, A. Ghezzi, and T. Buganza. 2021b. "Idle Asset Hunters— The Secret of Multi-Sided Platforms." *Research-Technology Management* 64, no. 1, pp. 33–42.

Chapter 6

Knapp, J., J, Zeratsky, and B. Kowitz. 2016. *Sprint: How to Solve Big Problems and Test New Ideas in Just Five Days.* New York, NY: Simon and Schuster.

Press, J., P. Bellis, T. Buganza, S. Magnanini, D. Trabucchi, A.B.R. Shani, R. Verganti, and F.P. Zasa. 2021. *IDeaLs (Innovation and Design as Leadership): Transformation in the Digital Era.* Bingley: Emerald Group Publishing.

Verganti, R. 2018. *Overcrowded: Designing Meaningful Products in a World Awash With Ideas.* Boston: MIT Press.

Chapter 7

Gallagher, L. 2017. *The Airbnb Story: How Three Guys Disrupted an Industry, Made Billions of Dollars... and Plenty of Enemies*. New York, NY: Random House.

Haidt, J. April 11, 2022. "Why the Past 10 Years of American Life Have Been Uniquely Stupid." *The Atlantic*.

Iansiti, M. and K.R. Lakhani. 2017. "Managing Our Hub Economy." *Harvard Business Review* 10.

Sanasi, S., D. Trabucchi, E. Pellizzoni, and T. Buganza. 2022. "The Evolution of Meanings: An Empirical Analysis of the Social Media Industry." *European Journal of Innovation Management* 25, no. 6, pp. 97–121.

Trabucchi, D., A. Moretto, T. Buganza, and A. MacCormack. 2020. "Disrupting the Disruptors or Enhancing Them? How Blockchain Reshapes Two-Sided Platforms." *Journal of Product Innovation Management* 37, no. 6, pp. 552–574.

Trabucchi, D., E. Pellizzoni, T. Buganza, and R. Verganti. 2017. "Interplay Between Technology and Meaning: How Music Majors Reacted?." *Creativity and Innovation Management* 26, no. 4, pp. 327–338.

Tully, S. June 20, 2019. "Tech's 4 Biggest Cash Burners Have Torn Through $23.9 Billion Combined." *Fortune*.

Zuboff, S. 2019. *The Age of Surveillance Capitalism*. London: Profile Books.

About the Authors

Daniel Trabucchi is senior assistant professor at the School of Management, Politecnico di Milano. He also serves as a senior researcher in the LEADIN'Lab, the Laboratory for LEAdership, Design, and INnovation. His research interests are focused on innovation management, especially digital two-sided platforms and digital services.

He cofounded Symplatform in 2018, the international conference on digital platforms that aims to match scholars and practitioners in the field.

He cofounded and is scientific director of Platform Thinking HUB, the community of innovation leaders that aims to foster innovation through platform thinking, which is part of the Digital Innovation Observatories of Politecnico di Milano. He is also scientific director of IDeaLs, the global research platform founded by Politecnico di Milano aiming to develop innovative ways to engage people in transformation processes.

He is a member of the scientific committee of the International Product Development Management Conference EIASM-IPDMC.

He has authored more than 70 scientific articles, including peer-reviewed journal articles, conference proceedings, and book chapters. His research has been published in relevant and recognized peer-reviewed journals such as *Journal of Product Innovation Management*, *Technological Forecasting and Social Change*, *R&D Management*, *International Journal of Entrepreneurial Behavior and Research*, *Internet Research*, *Research-Technology Management*, *Creativity and Innovation Management*, *Technology Analysis and Strategic Management*, and *European Journal of Innovation Management*; he is also a reviewer for many of these journals.

Apart from academic research, he teaches innovation and project management at various levels, from bachelor's to master's, MBAs, executive MBAs, and corporate classes, being also Director of the International Part Time MBA of the POLIMI Graduate School of Management. Moreover, he is often involved in advisory projects with small and multinational organizations in innovation and transformation management.

Contact Details:
daniel.trabucchi@polimi.it

QR code for Daniel Trabucchi's Linkedin profile: bit.ly/PT_Trabucchi.

Tommaso Buganza is full professor of Leadership & Innovation at the School of Management, Politecnico di Milano. He is also cofounder of LEADIN'Lab, the Laboratory for LEAdership, Design, and INnovation. He is a lecturer in innovation management and project management, responsible for the Project Management Academy, and coordinator of the innovation and training area at POLIMI Graduate School of Management. He teaches innovation management, project management, and organizational behavior at various levels, from bachelors to MBAs, executive MBAs, and corporate classes.

He is the chairman of the International Product Development Management Conference EIASM-IPDMC.

He cofounded Symplatform in 2018, the international conference on digital platforms that aims to match scholars and practitioners in the field.

He confounded and is scientific director of Platform Thinking HUB, the community of innovation leaders that aims to foster innovation through platform thinking, which is part of the Digital Innovation Observatories of Politecnico di Milano. Morevoer, he cofounded and is scientific director of IDeaLs, the global research platform founded by Politecnico di Milano aiming to develop innovative ways to engage people in transformation processes.

He has authored more than 100 scientific articles, including peer-reviewed journal articles, conference proceedings, and book chapters. His research has been published in relevant and recognized peer-reviewed journals such *as Journal of Product Innovation Management, Technological Forecasting and Social Change, Research-Technology Management,*

Creativity and Innovation Management, Technology Analysis and Strategic Management, International Journal of Project Management, and *European Journal of Innovation Management*; he is also a reviewer for many of these journals.

Contact Details:

tommaso.buganza@polimi.it

QR code for Tommaso Buganza's Linkedin profile: bit.ly/PT_Buganza.

Index

OTHER TITLES IN THE SERVICE SYSTEMS AND INNOVATIONS IN BUSINESS AND SOCIETY COLLECTION

Jim Spohrer, IBM and Haluk Demirkan, University of Washington, Tacoma, Editors

- *Servitization* by Antonio Pérez Márquez
- *Evolving With Inclusive Business in Emerging Markets* by Rajagopal
- *Hidden Challenges* by Elizabeth Florent Treacy, Fernanda Pomin, James Hennessy, Ricardo Senerman and Ross Emerson
- *Service in the AI Era* by Jim Spohrer, Paul P. Maglio, Stephen L. Vargo and Markus Warg
- *The Emergent Approach to Strategy* by Peter Compo
- *Emerging FinTech* by Paul Taylor
- *The Vice Chairman's Doctrine* by Ian Domowitz
- *Compassion-Driven Innovation* by Nicole Reineke, Hanna Yehuda and Debra Slapak
- *Adoption and Adaption in Digital Business* by Keith Sherringham and Bhuvan Unhelkar
- *Customer Value Starvation Can Kill* by Gautam Mahajan and Walter Vieira
- *ATOM, Second Edition* by Kartik Gada
- *Designing Service Processes to Unlock Value, Third Edition* by Joy M. Field
- *Disruptive Innovation and Digital Transformation* by Marguerite L. Johnson
- *Build Better Brains* by Martina Muttke

Concise and Applied Business Books

The Collection listed above is one of 30 business subject collections that Business Expert Press has grown to make BEP a premiere publisher of print and digital books. Our concise and applied books are for…

- Professionals and Practitioners
- Faculty who adopt our books for courses
- Librarians who know that BEP's Digital Libraries are a unique way to offer students ebooks to download, not restricted with any digital rights management
- Executive Training Course Leaders
- Business Seminar Organizers

Business Expert Press books are for anyone who needs to dig deeper on business ideas, goals, and solutions to everyday problems. Whether one print book, one ebook, or buying a digital library of 110 ebooks, we remain the affordable and smart way to be business smart. For more information, please visit www.businessexpertpress.com, or contact sales@businessexpertpress.com.